THE HITCHHIKERS GUIDE

GUIDE

to the

MEANING

of

EVERYTHING

WILLIAM BADKE

Kregel
Publications

Library of Congress Cataloging-in-Publication Data
Badke, William B.
   The hitchhiker's guide to the meaning of everything/by William Badke.
      p. cm.
      1. Bible—Criticism, interpretation, etc. I. Title.
BS511.3.B33   2005   220.6—dc22   2005022165

ISBN 0-8254-2069-5

Contents

Preface

You've been wondering what it's all about—who you are in the scheme of things, why you're here, how you can find happiness. Maybe you've been feeling empty lately or you've been hungering for something more than what life has offered you so far. It happens to all of us eventually, that nagging suspicion that our dreams aren't running on the same track as our reality.

I remember a time when, with a fresh university B.A., I wandered penniless for five months looking for anyone who would give me a job. "You're overqualified," people would tell me. "Nobody wants you."

It took me the whole five months finally to conclude that you can dream all you want, but life can suck the vital juices out of you and leave you a shriveled wreck in the dust. I survived that time and learned a few things in the process, but I'll never forget asking the silent heavens why the answers to the big questions of life are so elusive. I'm sure you're familiar with the longing that lives in the gap between what you want and what you have. If you think about it long enough, that longing can devour you.

The really ironic thing is that the answer to your longing may be lodged in a book already on your shelf attracting dust bunnies. That is where I found it. Funny how we would be willing to go off to India or even to some local guru if we could find some answers, when the solution to our quest could well be as close as our own bookshelf.

Don't let me hold you in suspense. This book that you are reading is about the Bible. I believe that ancient volume—the Bible—contains the secret to the meaning of life.

Now I know you may be thinking that the Bible is the last place anyone would want to look for new answers. The Bible is dusty and old.

Can something written that long ago mean anything to someone with a computer and a cell phone?

I think it can. I think it can turn your life around.

Before we go any further, though, I want to make you a promise— I'm not going to go into the old, tired routine of trying to *prove* to you that God exists, that he created the world, that miracles really do happen, or that everything the Bible has to say is completely true. Those are things you need to figure out for yourself.

What I want to do instead is tell you the Bible's story and introduce you to what the Bible has to say about your life on this earth. I want to reveal the message that has made such a difference in my own life. If you don't like what you read, then chuck the book. If you do like it, read on. What do you have to lose?

We live in an age that many people call "postmodern." One of the first postmodern novels ever written is a terrific source for understanding why we need something like the Bible if we're going to make sense of our own journey. The story goes something like this:

When Arthur Dent from the West Country region of England plunked himself down in the mud in front of the yellow bulldozer that was about to demolish his house, he had no idea how useless his gesture was going to be. In exactly twelve minutes, Planet Earth would be blasted to bits to make way for an alien hyperspatial express route.

Thus begins Douglas Adams's radio series, novel series, and now major motion picture, *The Hitchhiker's Guide to the Galaxy*, a bizarre romp through space in search of the meaning of life. Arthur, rescued by an extraterrestrial who had taken the unfortunate name Ford Prefect, eventually learned that many millions of years before, a computer had been set in motion to find "the answer to the great question of Life, the Universe, and Everything."

Seven-and-a-half million years later, the result came back, though the computer warned everyone that they wouldn't like it. The beings who had been waiting for so long begged, "Tell us the answer to the great question of Life, etc.," so the computer hesitantly did so. The answer was . . .

42.

42? What was 42? After all this time, all this waiting and anxiety, was this the best that the universe's greatest computer could come up with? It made no sense at all.

"*Of course it didn't,*" the computer informed them. How could it? The answer was definitely 42, but the seekers hadn't formulated the right question. When they identified the question, the answer would make sense. So they built another computer to find the question and called it "earth."

I won't give away the rest, but the point is simply this—for many of us, the quest for the meaning of life seems doomed to a lot of wasted time and a solution that makes no sense when we find it. Depressing, don't you think? Amusing, sure, but then there's that kicker at the end.

I suspect that you already know that searching for the meaning of life, the one meaning that all of us can take as our own, could be one of the biggest challenges you'll ever face. The meaning of life falls in line with the quest for truth, and few people have a clear sense of where truth can be found anymore, at least not truth that all of us can agree on.

We live in a world in which both meaning and truth have fallen on hard times. It's not that the truth may not be out there somewhere (as *X-Files* has taught us), but how do we discover what key to turn or what question to ask to find it?

Many people believe that the best way to come up with answers for themselves is to create their own spirituality. If we are thinking beings, even spiritual beings, why would we be content with buying into someone else's explanation of things, accepting their version instead of ours? If no way of thinking, or even of worshiping, is better than any other, why not go with our own beliefs? Everywhere there are gurus calling to us, "Walk this way. . . . No, walk this way," but who knows what's valid and what's not? Better just to trust our own instincts.

Not to be tied down to someone else's belief system could actually be a good thing. There is a special kind of freedom in being liberated from other people's creeds so you can forge new paths and locate your view of the world in the things that you find the most important.

But making your own spirituality does have its struggles. Sure, there are guidebooks you can buy to help you plot your journey, but who knows if they'll make sense or work for you? Even when you finally come up with an explanation that you can use, there is always a nagging fear that you're missing something, that the real answer is still out there, and your life will be greatly diminished if you don't find it. And always there is that troubling question: *Why am I here anyway?*

Ah, there's a question. A real question. The answer to it, according to *The Hitchhiker's Guide to the Galaxy,* is 42, which makes no sense. (*Why am I here?* 42. Do you see the problem?)

Maybe we're on the wrong track, believing that a computer built by mere human beings could find the ultimate answer. Maybe the answer isn't 42 or any other solution we could think of with our own limited minds. Even if we pooled all our consciousnesses together, maybe we still wouldn't have the explanation for our existence.

I don't think it's accurate to say, as *The Hitchhiker's Guide to the Galaxy* does, that we have a solution without a question. I think we do know what the question is. It's "Why am I here?" which means, *"Am I just some accident of history, or is the fact that I am a living, breathing human being something that is important in a grander scheme of things? Am I significant? Is there reason to believe I have value?"* The problem is that any sure answer seems to escape us.

If you're getting tired of uncertainty because no one can verify that any of the spiritualities out there (or the one you've made for yourself) can answer your deepest question, may I humbly suggest that you go back to something that is possibly sitting on a shelf somewhere in your own home—the Bible.

I don't know where you are with the Bible. Maybe you believe most of what it says, but you would like to have a fresh look at its message. Maybe you think it's a pack of nonsense, but you feel like you owe it to yourself to have somebody explain the nonsense before you dismiss it forever. Maybe you just don't know what to think.

Let me hand you an invitation: If you read on, I'll take you into the world of the Bible, not with the trappings of churches and theologies and rules that make you feel like a degenerate soul, but with the message as it's expressed right on the printed page. I'll try not to bore you, and I'll let you see the words of the Bible as I discuss them so you can decide whether it's saying what I claim it's saying.

If you come with me on this journey, we'll agree on one thing—you don't have to believe any of it if you don't want to. I'll take you through what it says, and you can make up your own mind. No pressure.

Bottom line: I think it's possible to show you the meaning of life, and it's not 42. If you buy into what I'm telling you, great. If not, at least you had a chance to look at this ancient book and decide it's not for you.

Why didn't I choose some other old scripture, like the Koran or the Upanishads? Not because I want to reject anybody else's faith but because I've found something in the Bible that I can't find anywhere else—a voice that comes from outside, a voice that speaks words that help me understand my life.

If you're tired of do-it-yourself everything, take a walk with me through a book that didn't come from either you or me. You'll likely find the journey interesting, and the payoff could be fabulous.

At this point, you might be saying to yourself, "Why waste my time looking for the meaning of life when there's likely nothing out there to find? Instead of reading this book, I could be doing any number of things to enjoy what I already have."

I have a friend who would have said the same thing. She grew up in a tough home with lots of problems and tells me she always felt like a stranger, as if she had been an alien baby parachuted into a human family. All her life she dreamed of finding an answer to whatever it was she was looking for, which wasn't the strife and confusion that troubled her. But her search led to nothing.

Then one summer she discovered herself in a job surrounded by people who took the Bible seriously. It was a strange environment for her at first, but gradually she noticed that she was paying attention to what these people had to say. She started reading this Bible her coworkers were talking about. And gradually, as she read, everything started to make sense, as if she had finally found her real family. She tells me it felt like coming home.

We live in a world without guideposts where it's easy to feel like a stranger far from the place where love and safety can be found. The Bible, I believe, forms a portal into that place, a doorway into eternal realities where our true home lies. If you read on, you could encounter everything you've been looking for. You could find your home.

If you read on, you could even discover the meaning of your life.

1

It Starts Here . . .

In the beginning God . . . (Genesis 1:1)

Many people like to make a big deal of the first four words of the Bible, as if "In the beginning God . . ." were saying something profound.

I suppose you could call it profound—before anything existed, God was already there, a steady Presence in the universe who didn't need to be there, but simply was. The Bible makes it clear that God is not a creation of human beings nor even a terribly explainable being. He simply is and has always been a gigantic Personality that predates everything else. Yet, when you think about it this is exactly who God would need to be if he were actually a voice from outside who could give us certainty.

There are lots of other possible gods we could create in our imaginations: We could say there is no God, and we're all here by some fluke; we could believe there are many gods who create chaos because each of them has a different agenda; we could imagine a god who isn't really a god because everything is god; or a god who is out there but has chosen not to reveal himself/itself. So many choices, so little certainty.

But here is a book, the Bible. It has a long history and millions of people who have believed it. What's more, it tells us from the start that God was here before we were, before anything was, a vast Personality who needed nothing and no one to help him keep on being. It's intriguing to consider the possibility of Someone that immensely significant when all that the world can tell us is that reality is something we have to make for ourselves.

You don't have to buy into everything the Bible teaches just to have a look at what it says about God. A book with such a long history that a number of otherwise intelligent people believe is likely worth a look before we dismiss it and move on. It claims to give certainty. No less a person than Jesus, in the later part of this book, declared, "You will know the truth, and the truth will set you free" (John 8:32). In a world with far too many voices, that is an attractive goal—to find something you can trust.

And so, let's spend a while checking out this God of the Bible. Let's watch him in action in the pages of this ancient book and see what we can make of him. Is the message about him consistent? Does he make sense? Is he believable? Can he actually tell us who we are?

The very beginning of the first book in the Bible—Genesis—gives us an introduction to him with its first words: "*In the beginning God . . .*" There he is, a Presence so much at the foundation of everything that he can exist without our help or knowledge; a Presence so powerful that nothing else would have existed unless he brought it into being.

The rest of this first sentence of the Bible is important too: "In the beginning God created the heavens and the earth." What it's telling us is not especially complicated—in the beginning, this God who was already there brought into being everything else. Genesis makes the claim that God is ultimately responsible for the fact that there is a world, a universe, a you and me.

You may find lurking within you a suspicion that something like this must be the explanation. You look at a flower or a puppy or the mountains or the ocean, and you wonder how chance could produce things of such beauty. Ugly and indifferent things you could understand, but beauty?

And so the Bible boldly states that in the beginning it was God who put his blueprint on everything he made, not just knitting together creatures and environment so they could merely do their job (whatever that was supposed to be), but creating art in the process.

God spoke and light shone in the sky. He spoke and the earth formed itself. He spoke and the plants and animals came into being. At every point, the words that he uttered were perfectly matched by the thing that he made so that chance didn't enter the equation at all. There were no mistakes, no botched efforts.

Surely it must seem like a fairy tale, but a very good one. Once you start here, with a God who created it all, who knows where you could go?

2

The Man on the Dumpster

I could hear the man's cries of pain from across the emergency ward while I waited for the doctor to patch my son's knee, torn up by a fall from his bike. This noisy guy switched back and forth between demanding service and shouting, "Don't! That hurts!" His problem? He'd fallen off a dumpster and hurt his arm. A dumpster. What was a heavily intoxicated man doing on top of a dumpster in the middle of the night? Maybe hoping to sleep in it or planning to root through it for his next meal?

You might have a tendency to distance yourself from people like this, pretend that they don't really belong in your environment, or tell yourself that they should get a grip. But what if you *were* this man, down on his luck, struggling to cope with what has turned out to be an angry planet? Would you feel like a stranger? Would you expect people to despise you? Could you hope that anybody at all would accept you as a person like other persons?

Maybe you identify with this fellow more than you would be willing to admit. Breaking in, belonging, finding community—all of those things are challenges. You want to be connected, but too often you know that behind those faces that seem to accept you are strangers who can't even begin to understand what is really going on in your soul. I've been there, like the person who walks into a saloon in a western and the piano stops playing and everyone stops to stare, while a chorus of unheard voices says, "There's no welcome for you here."

There is an answer to loneliness and alienation, though. It comes from the Bible, which tells us that we are bound together by a single reality—that all of us are made in the image of God. Here's what it says:

> *And the Lord God formed a man's body from the dust of the*
> *ground and breathed into it the breath of life. And the man*
> *became a living person. (Genesis 2:7)*

If this is an accurate reading of our origins, who are we? We are human, the Bible says. We are unique in the midst of creation, created not to abuse it (as we will see) but to take our place within it as creatures from a common ancestor.

This is an immense concept, even revolutionary. What divides you from the man on the dumpster or the person down the street who, by birth or circumstance, sees you as an outsider? Nothing, because no matter what that man or woman next to you thinks, you are as human as he or she is. If we want to begin identifying the meaning to life, surely it must lie here—in who we are. The Bible says we are human, fashioned by God from a single set of parents, our true mother and father.

To know that you are human is much more of a step toward understanding your purpose in life than you might think. Why? Because encompassed in the Bible's careful explanation of your humanity is enough to tell you that you are not only human but significant. The Bible is saying that you have a clear place in this world that is yours and cannot be taken from you, even if you find yourself living in a trash container.

According to Genesis, we were made out of the dust of the earth, not a very promising beginning and certainly not the kind of building material that would be likely to produce anything more than clay statues for the animals to knock over. What made us human, the Bible says, is that God breathed into us, giving us the essence of whatever we describe as "life." We became living souls, breathing, as it were, with the lungs of God, with the blood that he infused into us, with the flesh that he created out of dirt.

You might think this means that we are gods, the Creator having passed his essence onto us by breathing into us and making us divine. The man on the dumpster is my brother because he is only a god in disguise, just like me.

But the Bible doesn't go that direction, much as it would be great to imagine ourselves as divine creatures. It says, to be sure, that God breathed into us the essence of life, his life, but he still viewed us as creatures, with the physical properties of creatures and DNA that differs only a few percentage points from mice (an ironic reality if you read the ending of *The Hitchhiker's Guide to the Galaxy*).

So what do you make of the Bible's version of our origin on the earth? You could argue that it has been refuted by evolution, but remember that we're not debating about truth here, just trying to understand the Bible's vision of reality.

If you want to talk about evolution, you should recognize that it does nothing to define what is human. According to evolution, we are all what famed zoologist and author Desmond Morris called "naked apes." According to evolution, it is possible for humanity to have come from several origins, so that if your skin is black, you may not be exactly the same kind of human as one whose skin is white. This, of course, is contradicted by DNA evidence. The whole science of DNA, in fact, makes much better sense if all of us have a common origin. But then, we're not debating about truth right now, just making sense of the Bible's version of it.

The Bible's version tells us that humanity is a unity, specially formed by God and given the breath of life from his own nostrils.

It tells us that we are creatures with a unique origin, and all of us come from one set of parents. That is why I believe the man on the dumpster is my brother.

There is one more thing—God made us excellently. The end of the first chapter of the Bible goes like this:

> So God created people in his own image;
> God patterned them after himself;
> male and female he created them.

> God blessed them and told them, "Multiply and fill the earth and subdue it. Be masters over the fish and birds and all the animals." And God said, "Look! I have given you the seed-bearing plants throughout the earth and all the fruit trees for your food. And I have given all the grasses and other green plants to the animals and birds for their food." And so it was. Then God looked over all he had made, and he saw that it was excellent in every way. This all happened on the sixth day.
> (Genesis 1:27–31)

God looked at everything he had made and declared it excellent in every way, completely good. We weren't formed as messed up and broken creatures. We were not made inferior or twisted or evil. God created us according to his blueprint and shaped us perfectly, all of us.

We are connected because we come from a common source—our first parents made by God himself.

3

Special

Then God said, "Let us make people in our image, to be like ourselves. They will be masters over all life—the fish in the sea, the birds in the sky, and all the livestock, wild animals, and small animals." (Genesis 1:26)

In the ancient world, the great kings understood that they could only exert their control over the far-flung corners of their kingdoms if they could leave reminders of their presence everywhere. There was no CNN to keep all the citizens aware of who was in charge, so the kings left statues of themselves in prominent places all over their territories. They called these statues "images." Their purpose was simple—to leave visible reminders in the land of the one who ruled it so that people would think twice before they elected their own local rival king.

The Bible says, without hesitation, that we humans were made in the image of God. Since God does not by nature have a body and declares himself to be a spirit, the image of God has nothing to do with physical resemblance. If we buy into the idea that the Creator breathed into us, transforming us from dirt into living flesh, then something of him must be in us. This can't be his actual essence, his goodness, because only he is God and we are human. Yet the Bible says that we are somehow a reflection of him.

Language is a good example. There are many languages in the world, with a wide variety of structures, yet we can translate from one to another. We know that dolphins and whales, even pet dogs, know how to communicate, but they don't have the power to think in words, to transform those words into representations that we call writing, to communicate great complexities with one another and understand them. Language makes us special on this planet.

Since God is a communicating God, he wants to tell us things that we need to know. He wants to converse with us and us with him. This is really significant, because if language comes from God and his mind corresponds to ours, this gives humans the means to do more than simply experience the supernatural in some vague way—it gives them the opportunity to encounter the supernatural with their whole person—intellect, emotion, even will. It gives them a chance to talk to God and have the mysterious Creator talk to them. It gives them a chance to understand the things they would normally only have intuitions about.

If he has provided us with language, we know that he is a personal God. What do I mean by "personal"? We only understand the concept of personality because human beings are personal with characteristics like intellect, feeling, and the ability to take action. But if we have been created in the image of God, as a reflection of the Creator, then our minds, our emotions, our wills, all the things that make us "persons," must originate from God. We know he is personal because he made us in his image and we are personal.

The Bible abounds with the reality that God, as mysterious as he is, can't be seen as an impersonal presence or a force but as a personality. From the beginning of Genesis we find God speaking: *"Let there be light,"* and there is light; *"Let there be plants,"* and there are plants.

The Creator also carries a full range of emotions. Psalm 103:8 tells us:

> *The Lord is merciful and gracious;*
> *he is slow to get angry and full of unfailing love.*

But we're only scratching the surface here, admiring the king's statue and remarking on how much it looks like the king, as if resemblance were the most import thing. It's not. We haven't yet considered why the statue is there. Genesis 1:26 starts, "Let us make people in our image," then goes on to say, "They will be masters over all life—the fish in the sea, the birds in the sky, and all the livestock, wild animals, and small animals."

Before you get all giggly at the prospect of being given permission by God to be a king or queen so you can dominate the rest of the life forms on earth and use them for your pleasure, let's take stock. Who rules? Well, God, if he made all things as the Bible claims. He rules totally, without rival, because he was there before anything was made. Nothing made him. If we've been given any opportunity to rule, then we have it by permission, under his authority.

This is where that image concept goes deeper than resemblance. The Bible is claiming that we were put on this earth to *represent* God as rulers under his supreme command. In our very creation in the image of God, the intention was that we were to stand as visible reminders to all other creatures that God is king. In this way we "image" him by being his representatives in the created order. We are to rule, but only in recognition that God rules us and we work for him.

How does God rule? Certainly not by abusing and exploiting the world. Why would the one who made something so full of splendor, beauty, complexity, and mystery turn around and treat it like a banquet to devour? If you formed this world, would you set your highest creation loose to vandalize it?

In the statements within the first couple of chapters of the Bible, then, we've already been given an inkling of what the Bible claims God made us for. By bearing a resemblance to his character, we were created to represent his presence and stand as "images" in the world, telling all creation that God rules and we rule under his command, fulfilling his purposes in the world.

Something else echoes through what the Bible has to say about the creation of human beings. It's simply this—God made human beings to be like him so that he could have a relationship with them beyond that of anything else he created. He wanted to connect with them. He wanted them to find him and know him as well as he can be known. He had no intention of hiding himself. The very fact that we are made in his image means that the possibility of knowing him is built into our very existence on this earth.

We are special because we have a special connection with the One who made us.

4

Craving Community

Community is a big deal these days, especially in a society where feeling personally isolated and lonely is one of our greatest burdens. It's pretty clear to most that we need other people in our lives if we want to be whole. In fact, medical research tells us that men and women who are isolated from others have poorer health and die younger than those who have vibrant communities within which they can experience a strong sense of belonging.

Some experts on human life explain this craving for community pretty simply: As we evolved, they say, we discovered that isolation was a quick way to have someone steal our food or murder us. There was risk in solitude but safety in numbers. Humans learned to flock together to find security. Since the fear of being alone and vulnerable was so primal and powerful, we've carried it along, generation after generation, so that it sticks with us even today, when it's possible to be more or less self-sufficient. This ancient terror is what still drives us together.

But that explanation won't cover everything. You see, people don't just seek community because it's risky to be alone. We crave each other's company because we value it, and we wither and die unless we have others who are a significant part of our world, even when we feel perfectly safe and have our every physical need met. Why is that?

The Bible says it's because we were made to need community and could not find fulfillment without it:

> *So God created people in his own image;*
> *God patterned them after himself;*
> *male and female he created them.*

*And the Lord God said, "It is not good for the man to be alone. I
will make a companion who will help him." So the Lord God
formed from the soil every kind of animal and bird. He brought
them to Adam to see what he would call them, and Adam chose
a name for each one. He gave names to all the livestock, birds,
and wild animals. But still there was no companion suitable for
him. (Genesis 1:27; 2:18–20)*

In our basic design, we were created in God's image as male and
female. Most would agree that as soon as you have males and females
they are going to gravitate into community. Thus, our creation as gen-
ders means we're going to relate to each other by instinct

But there is more. When Adam was first made, he was the only
human on earth. And God saw that he had no one who corresponded
to him. Such a situation was, by its very existence, "not good," even
though everything else in creation was "good." Why? Because God had
made the man so that community was a basic need built into the human
make-up.

Adam couldn't go on being alone, not just because he couldn't bear
children by himself, but because he couldn't survive his isolation. It was
not natural. He had been constructed for community. The animals
couldn't provide his communal needs, or he would have been content
with them. Only another person could satisfy him.

*So the Lord God caused Adam to fall into a deep sleep. He took
one of Adam's ribs and closed up the place from which he had
taken it. Then the Lord God made a woman from the rib and
brought her to Adam. (Genesis 2:21–22)*

When God made the woman, he didn't scoop her out of the dirt like
he had with Adam. Instead, God took her out of the very substance of
Adam himself, not so he could forever claim some sort of superiority,
but so Adam could understand that she was bone of his bone, flesh of
his flesh. So that Adam could grasp that he was part of a community
constructed of those who were so much like him that they were him.
Thus he was as responsible for her as he was for himself, because she
came from him. So we read:

*"At last!" Adam exclaimed. "She is part of my own flesh and
bone! She will be called 'woman,' because she was taken out of a*

> *man." This explains why a man leaves his father and mother*
> *and is joined to his wife, and the two are united into one. Now,*
> *although Adam and his wife were both naked, neither of them*
> *felt any shame. (Genesis 2:23–25)*

The explanation of some is that we are driven together because we are vulnerable when we are alone. The explanation of the Bible is that we need, we *crave*, community, because community is built into our very nature. In a world that is longing for bonds that will complete us and end our aching loneliness, God says, "It's not good to be alone."

Another thing, and this is the start of a deep mystery: The Bible claims that when God first pronounced the fact that he was going to create humanity, he said, "Let *us* create man in *our* image" (Genesis 1:26 NIV, emphasis added). Who is "us"? Is this just God's fancy way of speaking, like a "royal we"? Or do we have here a clue that there is community in humanity (made in God's image) because there is community in God?

Here's one more juicy tidbit in the Genesis version of our creation. Sex, within the bounds of a forever relationship, is not only tolerated by God but encouraged and celebrated, not just so children can be born but because it bonds us within community. Who would have thought it?

5

Some Kind of Test

I once watched a sitcom whose hero lived an utterly gray life—no parties, never a joke on his lips. Why? Life, he explained, seeks equilibrium. If you have a good time, then an equal and opposite bad time will soon come along and bite you. Better to live in the gray middle and avoid the pain, because life's equalizing program will make you pay for every pleasure you enjoy.

Life does seem constantly to be seeking equilibrium. In Genesis 2 we have a further account of the story of creation by an all-wise Maker. We get a loving couple and a fabulous garden for them to live in. We even see an inkling of meaning for them. But no sooner do we get going down this road than we find there's a roadblock, a downside.

Let's start with the inkling of meaning.

We are told that God put the man into the Garden to care for it. In this, the Bible shows itself to be environmentally friendly—really. According to Genesis 2, when the first man was formed out of the dust of the ground in order to represent God's rule in the world, he was given a job. Quite simply, he was told to work the ground and keep the creation in order. God made it; Adam was supposed to tend it.

I know what you've heard about Bible believers—that they think they're better than the animals and trees, that they're behind the worst evils of Western civilization and have made the rest of the natural world a "consumable," something to be used to improve our standard of living, no matter what it costs in mayhem and destruction to the environment.

But the Bible says that God made the world, treasured every part of it, and gave humanity the responsibility of taking care of it—working and nurturing it so that it would shine in honor of the one who made it:

The Lord God placed the man in the Garden of Eden to tend and care for it. (Genesis 2:15)

Any notion that we humans were given permission to plunder God's world for our own amusement is dashed by the work God gave Adam to do.

Here's another direction for a possible meaning for our lives—the answer is not 42, but *work*. Work? Before you start groaning, just think about how much meaning we humans derive from work, not only the means to finance our needs and pleasures but our sense of personal value. Is it a mistake that personal accomplishment makes us feel significant?

Adam got more than just something to do when he was told to take care of the creation. The Creator gave him a personal sense of value. Adam was handed a place in the universe that couldn't be taken from him because it had been given to him by the one who made the universe. Surely there must be meaning a-plenty here.

But there were limits to the paradise Adam and Eve enjoyed in the Garden. No sooner did they find their place in the world than God set their boundaries:

The Lord God placed the man in the Garden of Eden to tend and care for it. But the Lord God gave him this warning: "You may freely eat any fruit in the garden except fruit from the tree of the knowledge of good and evil. If you eat of its fruit, you will surely die." (Genesis 2:15–17)

Sure, Adam and Eve could eat any fruit in the Garden, but God put an obstacle in the way—the tree of the knowledge of good and evil was off limits. If they ate from it, they would die. The fruit from this tree sounds like magic with a bite to it (if you'll excuse the pun). But before you start dismissing it as another one of those crazy creation stories about some mythical plant with the power to kill, let's get another take on it.

There was probably nothing magic about the fruit. Surprised? Well, let's reckon with the idea that Adam and Eve already knew "good," because "good," by definition, was whatever pleased God. If they chose "bad," say the disobedient act of eating fruit they were told not to eat, then they would know evil. "Evil," by definition, would be anything that God didn't like. If he made everything, he sets the rules. This means that getting to know good and evil needed no magic, just an act of defiance.

So this command seems to have been some kind of test: Eat what you like, but don't cross the line God drew in the sand. Eat all the fruit, but not *that* fruit. Why not? Because God makes the rules.

The proposed penalty was harsh—death. Really harsh, actually. When was the last time you threatened your child (or little sibling) with death if he or she stole from the cookie jar? Sure, if God created these people, he could remove them. But it's disturbing all the same to hear words like God speaks in Genesis 2. He seems to be saying, "Cross me, even once, and you die." So much for lovingly creating human beings in his image. The love only goes as far as their first act of disobedience.

Don't judge God too harshly, though, until you recognize that we may not yet be seeing the full picture. Give it time. Let's see how the story plays out.

6

A Bid for Liberation

*Now the serpent was the shrewdest of all the creatures the Lord
God had made. "Really?" he asked the woman. "Did God really
say you must not eat any of the fruit in the garden?" (Genesis 3:1)*

It all started well, but in the way life often seems to take us, things
went south really fast. We've already seen a problem—the strange prohibition that God set for Adam and Eve—but this was nothing compared with what happened when the serpent showed up.

This was a talking serpent, a creature obviously possessed by Satan
himself. He challenged the woman to rethink God's strange command
about the forbidden fruit. Imagine how the words, "Did God really
say . . . ?" rang through this perfect world where questioning God had
never before been contemplated. Maybe God needed to be questioned,
but that is something you'll have to work through later in the story. For
now, just imagine the shock it was to Eve:

*"Of course we may eat it," the woman told him. "It's only the
fruit from the tree at the center of the garden that we are not
allowed to eat. God says we must not eat it or even touch it, or
we will die." (Genesis 3:2–3)*

She answered like someone offended at the notion that anyone
would challenge the Creator. "It's true," she argued. "That's what he
said. In fact, he won't even let us touch it." This last part was tagged
on—something God never told her, but she had built up his command
in her mind and made it more than it was.

"You won't die!" the serpent hissed. "God knows that your eyes will be opened when you eat it. You will become just like God, knowing everything, both good and evil." (Genesis 3:4–5)

With bewildering speed, the serpent's message struck. "You won't die." In other words, he was telling her, "God's a liar. He said you would die, but you won't." God? The Maker? The One she had never doubted before? Why in the world would God want to lie to the people he had specially made?

"Simple," the serpent might have told her, probably already gloating over his coming triumph. "God has a secret. He knows that making people in his image has given them the potential to become just like him, and he doesn't want to share his power with anyone. God knows that if they break his rule and eat the fruit, it will unleash their power, and he won't be the Supreme One anymore. They'll know good and evil just like he does."

To people who feel comfortable with the idea of God's being in control, the serpent comes off like a monster breaking up a great relationship between the Creator and the people he made. But there are others who argue that the serpent was right—just because God lays claim to having created us, this doesn't mean he has the right to turn us into his slaves. Good point. Maybe being under God's power doesn't exactly appeal to you. Maybe we were made for something better. While some people call the events of Genesis 3 the fall of humanity, other people see it as humanity's liberation.

Since the jury is still out on that one, let's take a look for a moment at Eve, standing there listening to the serpent, her mouth open in astonishment. The chapter goes on:

> *The woman was convinced. The fruit looked so fresh and delicious,*
> *and it would make her so wise! So she ate some of the fruit.*
> *She also gave some to her husband, who was with her. Then he*
> *ate it, too. At that moment, their eyes were opened. . . . (Genesis 3:6–7)*

She stared at the fruit. It looked great (maybe it was an apple, like the stories say, or maybe a grapefruit; it doesn't matter). Eve clearly bought into the argument that the fruit would make her wise like God. So she ate it. She ate the fruit that God had told her not to eat, and she did it deliberately. Yet before you blame everything that followed on the woman, read the rest—Adam ate it too.

Did they know what they had done? They thought so. Was it liberation? I'll leave that for you to decide.

7

Adam, Where Are You?

Was eating the forbidden fruit a liberation or a disaster? Our opportunity to check out an answer to that question comes quickly. While it surely was a downer for public nudity, there is much more to the story:

> *At that moment, their eyes were opened, and they suddenly felt shame at their nakedness. So they strung fig leaves together around their hips to cover themselves.*
> *Toward evening they heard the Lord God walking about in the garden, so they hid themselves among the trees.*
> *The Lord God called to Adam, "Where are you?"*
> *He replied, "I heard you, so I hid.*
> *I was afraid because I was naked." (Genesis 3:7–10)*

Here is the situation—both the man and the woman had eaten the fruit that God commanded them not to eat, risking the promise of certain death if they defied him. But they didn't die, at least not in the way they had expected. The first thing they discovered was shame. Embarrassed about their nakedness, they quickly fashioned clothes for themselves.

It appears that God had a habit of taking a physical form and walking with them in the cool of the day, a sort of regular let's-stay-connected effort. Now, as they heard God taking his stroll in the Garden, they hid themselves, prompting God to ask, "Where are you?"

It seems like God knew exactly where Adam was, so the question was really intended to draw Adam out of hiding. If Adam's response to God's question is any indication, Adam knew he was busted—he showed himself right away, like you do when you're caught in a hide-and-go-seek game.

There might be something more significant in the "Where are you?" question if the Creator were saying, "Hey, Adam, now that you've eaten the fruit, where exactly are you in your quest for the meaning of life?"

So where were they, these brave, defiant ones?

Obviously, they were now like God, knowing good and evil. Then why, pray tell, were they hiding from God, cowering in the bushes? The answer has to have something to do with shame and fear. Had they become like God? Well, in many ways they had always been like him because they were created in his image.

Maybe the better question is this: Had they gained the power they were seeking? You tell me—are people cowering in the shrubbery empowered? Were they better than they had once been? Had they overcome the burden of servanthood and become their own people? Were they as powerful as the One who had made them?

I think not. But maybe they just hadn't yet grasped what they had accomplished. Perhaps it simply took time to realize that they were free of this Master, liberated to find their own identity in the world. Could be. Before we launch off too strongly in that direction, though, let's look at what they had gained or lost. The chapter goes on:

> "Yes," Adam admitted, "but it was the woman you
> gave me who brought me the fruit, and I ate it."
> Then the Lord God asked the woman,
> "How could you do such a thing?"
> "The serpent tricked me," she replied. "That's why I ate it."
> (Genesis 3:12–13)

What we find here is a bad case of alienation and denial. The nastiness that emerged sounds strangely familiar because we encounter the same thing in our own experience. To see their response is to see ours.

God says to Adam, "Did you eat the fruit?" and he replies, "The woman you put here with me, it's her fault." Surprise. Just before this time, he had called her bone of his bone and flesh of his flesh. Now she is some defective creature who has enticed him to do wrong. Imagine how she felt when she heard those words that turned love into accusation. You want a reason we're so alienated from one another? The Bible puts the source of all our interpersonal problems on the conflict that resulted from our first parents making a bid to challenge God.

And then there is the denial—Adam says it's not his fault, it's the woman's; the woman says it's not her fault, it's the serpent's.

Disturbing stuff. The first couple had hoped for liberation from their Creator so they could be their own people with powers as great as his, but this hope has now led to diminished, alienated people. Was it liberation? It doesn't look like liberation. Sure, maybe they would do better in the future when they learned how to handle their independence with more skill. But right then, things looked bad.

Comparing their scene with ours, we may see a similar picture. We, too, feel shame for things we have done. We experience fear and guilt. We tend to turn on one another and play the blame game. There is a lot of commonality between Genesis 3 and life as it's lived every day.

I would like to come right out and ask you a question to think about. You don't have to have an answer right away, but it nags at me as I read the account of Adam and Eve and their seemingly failed bid for freedom. Here it is: *If there is so little difference between Adam and Eve protesting in the Garden, and our own here-and-now experience, have you ever wondered if something might be fundamentally wrong with us? With me and with you? With all of us? Is something broken in the human race?*

I'm not trying to offend you, asking such a thing. If you're hurt by my suggestion, then let me ask another question: *From where does all the turmoil in our lives come?* That's easy—it comes from living among people. The famous existentialist author Jean-Paul Sartre put it this way: *"L'Enfer c'est les autres"* (Hell is other people). And it's true. The problem isn't you, it's people like me who get in your face, who misunderstand you and treat you in ways you don't deserve.

Ever wonder how all this started, how we developed such a capacity to hurt one another, to alienate ourselves from one another? Ever wonder why it's so hard for any of us to accept personal responsibility for our actions?

The Bible puts it back on eating forbidden fruit. In Adam and Eve, after their act of defiance, we don't find empowered people. We find diminished creatures. Adam turns on his wife, and his wife blames the serpent; nobody wants to let anything stick to them. They started so well, but now they seem much more like the people of our world, those we know and live with.

Could it be that these glorious creatures have become not like God, but like us?

8

Going on Down

"I think to myself, 'What a wonderful world!'" That's how Louis Armstrong put it in his song decades ago. He must have lived on a better planet than I do, without violence and hatred, without every kind of relationship meltdown imaginable, and death waiting around the next corner. My world doesn't look very wonderful.

All of us know that life and nasty episodes can go together as easily as bread and peanut butter. Sure, there is a lot to be happy about, but none of us escapes the pain that lurks around the corner. In fact, unexplainable trouble can mess us up so badly that we're ready either to deny there is a God or challenge him to justify the pain he has caused us.

Where did all this evil and trouble on our planet come from? The Bible says it started when the first people on earth made a bid for independence from the One who formed them. Later in the story of humanity, a man named Eliphaz would put it this way, his approach crude, but at least direct:

> *From my experience, I know that fools who turn from God may*
> *be successful for the moment, but then comes sudden disaster.*
> *Their children are abandoned far from help, with no one to*
> *defend them. Their harvests are stolen, and their wealth satisfies*
> *the thirst of many others, not themselves! But evil does not*
> *spring from the soil, and trouble does not sprout from the earth.*
> *People are born for trouble as predictably as sparks fly upward*
> *from a fire. (Job 5:3–7)*

According to Eliphaz, we are born for trouble. It's built into our experience from day one because we have turned from God.

God's response to the first couple's bid for independence was not pleasant; a classic example of tough love. Quite simply, the Creator took Adam and Eve out of their perfect existence and gave them something shabbier in its place.

> *Then he said to the woman, "You will bear children with intense*
> *pain and suffering. And though your desire will be for your*
> *husband, he will be your master." (Genesis 3:16)*

For Eve, it meant far greater pain in childbirth than had originally been planned. Beyond that, the rest of God's bad news for the first woman, though a bit hard to understand, appears to say that men would forcibly dominate women, a tragedy that plagues most cultures in the world.

> *And to Adam he said, "Because you listened to your wife and*
> *ate the fruit I told you not to eat, I have placed a curse on the*
> *ground. All your life you will struggle to scratch a living from*
> *it. It will grow thorns and thistles for you, though you will eat*
> *of its grains. All your life you will sweat to produce food, until*
> *your dying day. Then you will return to the ground from which*
> *you came. For you were made from dust, and to the dust you*
> *will return." (Genesis 3:17–19)*

In Adam's case, the environment that had completely met human needs without much effort on his part, would now produce only grudgingly. The ground was cursed so that it brought forth its treasures only if Adam farmed it like the dickens.

Questions abound. Is all the trouble in the world because God angrily gave us a raw deal? Is the Bible telling us that the world is cursed and doomed? Are we? The whole idea seems so negative that we have a lot of trouble dealing with it at all. Adam and Eve defied God, and he paid them back with tribulation.

To start making sense of God's judgment, we need to remember what he warned them would happen if they ate the fruit. If they ate it, they would die. They didn't die in the way you would expect. So maybe they should be grateful that God only increased their misery instead of killing them.

The only problem is that their misery appears to have become our misery, because the kind of judgment they received has filtered all the way down to us—pain, domination, and hard work for few results. We can be thankful God didn't wipe out the human race, but the judgment he did pass down seems to be too harsh a retribution for eating a piece of fruit.

Is all of this resonating with you? I want to know that the Bible's explanation makes sense in your own mind, even if its message is disturbing. Here it is in a nutshell:

The world is full of pain and trouble—any fool knows that, and you're no fool—just as much as it's full of beauty and wonder. The beauty and wonder makes sense if God created the world, but the trouble is more baffling. Into the mix of pain and wonder that is our experience, the Bible sends the message that the first humans were given a choice to have only beauty, but they bought into a rebellion they believed would make them like their Maker.

The results were alienation from one another and from God, denial of their own responsibility (neither of which can be blamed on God), and judgment on them from the Creator (which maybe can be seen as his fault). Shortly after, God sent them out of the Garden into a world that was not only harsh but also pretty final, because he cut them off from his presence.

Things were not going well for the first people on earth. Where once they might have said that their personal meaning of life was to recognize who made them and live joyfully and obediently in his presence, their whole purpose has now grown murky. Once they became rebels, who were they? According to the Bible, God was angry. Were they liberated? The Bible and the mocking voice of human tragedy all around us say they weren't and we're not.

They ate a piece of fruit and brought tragedy on themselves. It's almost too baffling for words that such a tiny act should change them so profoundly and bring such a heavy judgment down on their heads.

Was this the end of hope for any kind of positive relationship with God? Given our new doubts about his fairness in passing judgment on humanity, would we even want a relationship with a deity who appears to have turned against us?

9

Murder Just Outside of Paradise

When Michael Jackson was first arrested on sexual molestation charges in late 2003, a radio reporter went to the streets of Vancouver, B.C., to ask Michael's fans if their view of him had changed. Not surprisingly, many said the police were wrong and Michael was innocent. But some made the point that what you do is not at all the same as what you are. Even if Michael did this crime, it doesn't necessarily mean he is a bad person. When you love his music, what does his private life have to do with anything?

There is a certain logic to that. Good people regularly do things they're ashamed of, but they still go on functioning as pretty good people. Nobody is perfect, and so maybe our deeds don't really define us; they just prove that people are complex, and the best of us blow it every once in a while.

But here's the struggle—at what point do you stop cutting a person some slack and start thinking, "This is a bad dude." Let's try an extreme situation: Ted Bundy was a nice guy by most people's estimation. He really had only one annoying habit—periodically he would murder someone. In fact, before he was executed in 1989, he had killed dozens of women. Was he a good person who occasionally did bad things, or was there a fundamental flaw in the guy that made any good deeds he did simply beside the point?

I would much rather say that a person who does bad things is basically good with a few glitches. But even if we back off an extreme case like Ted Bundy and just consider an ordinary person who has lapses every once in awhile, we have to wonder what connection there is between who someone is and what that person does. Though it bothers me, I start to wonder if I blew up in anger at a friend because I was acting out of character or because that anger is built into my character, just needing the right spark to set it off.

In the case of Adam and Eve, something profound seems to have happened to them the moment they made their escape from God. It wasn't just that their actions showed they were going through a patch of trouble. The way they thought, even their characters, started on a transformation downward.

We have here a couple of people who gave up paradise for a chance at being gods. Their actions show evidence of having diminished them, bringing down the anger of the One who could do a lot to hurt them. So what do you think would happen when such people decided to breed? Let's read the account in the Bible:

> *Now Adam slept with his wife, Eve, and she became pregnant.*
> *When the time came, she gave birth to Cain, and she said,*
> *"With the Lord's help, I have brought forth a man!" Later she*
> *gave birth to a second son and named him Abel.*
> *When they grew up, Abel became a shepherd,*
> *while Cain was a farmer. At harvesttime Cain brought to the*
> *Lord a gift of his farm produce, while Abel brought several*
> *choice lambs from the best of his flock. The Lord accepted Abel*
> *and his offering, but he did not accept Cain and his offering.*
> *This made Cain very angry and dejected. (Genesis 4:1–5)*

Adam and Eve, according to the Bible, had two sons: Cain and Abel. Cain appears to have been a rough-edged character and Abel a good guy. One day, they both brought a sacrifice to God. The sacrifice was probably a good idea. Now that the family had been kicked out of the Garden of Eden, it was a wise move to reestablish ties with their Maker. A sacrifice would do the job. But God didn't accept what Cain had to offer. From what followed, it is likely that the rejection came from the fact that Cain was a less-than-perfect fellow who had a bad attitude. Whatever the reason, God found his sacrifice underwhelming. The story continues:

> *This made Cain very angry and dejected. . . .*
> *Later Cain suggested to his brother, Abel, "Let's go out into the*

fields." And while they were there, Cain attacked and killed his
brother. (Genesis 4:5, 8)

Cain couldn't get over the rejection of his sacrifice. While he stewed over it, his thoughts turned to a bad place. Maybe he believed he could win back favor with God if he got rid of the competition, maybe he was jealous, or maybe he wasn't thinking clearly at all. In any case, he decoyed his brother into a private place and killed him. Plain and simple, the Bible says the firstborn son on earth murdered the second.

So what on earth was going on with these people? It's one thing to eat forbidden fruit; it's another to slaughter your brother out of jealousy and revenge. Human life started so well. Now we have deception and murder, and we're hard pressed to explain how, within one generation, a family intent on liberation from their Maker could degenerate into this. Maybe Cain was just a bad apple, but we have to consider how someone who was one generation removed from perfection could commit premeditated murder on his own brother. We have to wonder how so much evil sprouted up so quickly.

Question: Did something nasty get passed on from Adam and Eve to their descendents? Is that what the Bible is telling us? Or let's ask it another way: Was the rebellion of Adam and Eve a much bigger deal than we've been thinking, sending a stream of corruption down the human line?

Now *there's* something none of us want to contemplate. If the potential for evil is passed on like a bad gene, then, according to the Bible, all of us must have it, because we all come from the same ancestors. The famous apostle Paul would later put it this way:

> *When Adam sinned, sin entered the entire human race.*
> *Adam's sin brought death, so death spread to everyone,*
> *for everyone sinned. (Romans 5:12)*

In that passage Paul used that uncomfortable word *sin,* describing Adam's bid to be like God, to be independent from the One who made him. That was the essence of *sin.*

Let's move a little farther along in Genesis 4 and meet a real beauty named Lamech:

> *One day Lamech said to Adah and Zillah,*
> *"Listen to me, my wives. I have killed a youth who attacked*

and wounded me. If anyone who kills Cain is to be punished
seven times, anyone who takes revenge against me will be
punished seventy-seven times!" (Genesis 4:23–24)

Lamech's favorite campfire song was a celebration of bloody revenge. A wound is paid back by murder. If vengeance is to be won against Cain, Lamech has won ten times that much vengeance and more. He lives to shed blood.

Maybe all of this is too dark for you. When I asked you to embark on a journey through the Bible, perhaps you thought I would simply be passing on a few happy thoughts to help you make it through this cruel world. Well, there are happy thoughts to come, for sure, but the Bible aims at doing no less than explaining the meaning of life. That means we need to come face to face with what it says about the dark side as well as the light.

What emerges is frightening. Not only did Adam and Eve's bid for independence apparently fail to liberate them, not only did it diminish them and leave them judged by their Maker, but there is a strong suspicion that some kind of corruption is working its way down from them into their offspring.

You might scoff at such a thought. You, after all, are undoubtedly a good person, no killer for sure. Likely you're trying to make your good deeds outweigh your bad deeds so you can look at yourself in the mirror without flinching. And for sure, you resist probing into the dark places in your own inner world where bad thoughts come from— thoughts of jealousy and lust and hatred that you show to no one.

But wait a minute—how do I know about your dark places? Because I have them too. We all do if we're breathing. A lot of spiritualities today tell us how to transcend ourselves and get connected. But none of them go as far as the Bible does to probe into our dark places. And none of them offers so much hope for a way to overcome whatever it is that lurks deep within our souls.

10

Footprints in the Mud

We're getting buried in misery here. What started as a glorious hope has turned into a series of reflections on life at its worst. There was a lot of promise for the human race to believe that being made in the image of God could help us become gods ourselves.

Now it seems like humanity has failed at its one attempt to find glory and has been judged and condemned. God, whoever he is, has walked away to leave us to our own devices, which seem pretty limited. Where's the hope in that? How do we find the meaning of life in being abandoned by the One who claims to have made us?

You'll have to forgive me. I wanted to spell out just how far down into the mud the Bible claims we've gone, but I've left out a few things—hints and whispers that we're not forgotten, footprints left behind by the same God who made us. What do I mean? Let's go back to the darkest moments of Genesis 3, in the midst of God's harsh words of condemnation after Adam and Eve bought into the serpent's lies and ate the forbidden fruit. The Creator cursed the serpent with the words:

> *So the Lord God said to the serpent, "Because you have done this, you will be punished. You are singled out from all the domestic and wild animals of the whole earth to be cursed. You will grovel in the dust as long as you live, crawling along on your belly. From now on, you and the woman will be enemies, and your offspring and her offspring will be enemies. He will crush your head, and you will strike his heel." (Genesis 3:14–15)*

What in the world is that about? I don't blame you for being puzzled. It would actually be centuries from the time it was written before it started to make sense, but for now let's consider it a promise—there would be enmity between the offspring of the serpent and the offspring of the woman.

Explaining our life's conflict with the serpent as simply an ongoing disgust with slithering creatures seems too trivial here. There has to be more. Later, in the time of Jesus, others would interpret it in terms of a royal battle between Satan and Christ in which Christ would destroy Satan's power. So maybe there's a hint of hope here that a victory awaits, a footprint of God in the mud of our existence.

Just a few sentences later, we find God doing the unbelievable:

> *And the Lord God made clothing from animal skins for Adam*
> *and his wife. (Genesis 3:21)*

Don't forget why Adam and Eve needed clothing. One of the first results of eating the forbidden fruit was that they experienced shame over their nakedness and hid from God. Now, instead of simply wiping them off the face of the earth, he replaced their hastily made clothing of leaves with animal skins. That meant God had to shed the blood of animals, made and treasured by him, to clothe a couple of rebels who had spurned his love. Another one of God's footprints in the mud, another sign that he's not done with us.

Then we come to Cain. After he brutally murdered his younger brother and was rightly banished by God, Cain had the audacity to complain. We read:

> *Cain replied to the Lord, "My punishment is too great for me to*
> *bear! You have banished me from my land and from your*
> *presence; you have made me a wandering fugitive. All who see*
> *me will try to kill me!"*
> *The Lord replied, "They will not kill you, for I will give seven*
> *times your punishment to anyone who does." Then the Lord put*
> *a mark on Cain to warn anyone who might try to kill him.*
> *(Genesis 4:13–15)*

God put a mark on Cain so that no one would be allowed to kill him. Why? Hard to say. Cain was a monster who hadn't shown an ounce of remorse for his evil slaughter of his brother. He deserved nothing, but God protected him from harm. Baffling, isn't it?

How about this? "Enoch lived 365 years in all. He enjoyed a close relationship with God throughout his life. Then suddenly, he disappeared because God took him" (Genesis 5:23–24). A man named Enoch, born into Adam's line, somehow recovered the experience of Eden and then wasn't there any more because God took him. Took him where? Presumably wherever God was—paradise, heaven. So here we have a man named Enoch who, in the midst of all this human turmoil, experienced what Adam had before his decision to become like God. He walked with the One who had made him. What's even more puzzling was that the same God who apparently banished the first humans from the Garden into a world of woe, welcomed a relationship with Enoch and finally took this man to be with him.

Or what about Noah? There is a story in Genesis 6–8 about God's purging the human race by wiping out most of it in a flood, saving only godly Noah and his family by means of an enormous floating zoo called an "ark." The purge failed because after the flood was over, Noah himself fell in love with the wine he made from his grapevines, and disgraced himself.

It was said of Noah (though presumably God knew he would later degenerate into an alcoholic stupor) that "Noah found favor with the Lord" (Genesis 6:8).

God preserved the human race through Noah and the ark. So the Bible says that God, who had every reason to destroy a humanity that had degenerated into an ungodly mess, chose to "refresh" the world of people by starting anew with a single family.

When Noah left the ark we find an amazing promise from the God who appeared to have abandoned the creatures he had made in his image. It's in Genesis 8:

> *Then Noah built an altar to the Lord and sacrificed on it the animals and birds that had been approved for that purpose. And the Lord was pleased with the sacrifice and said to himself, "I will never again curse the earth, destroying all living things, even though people's thoughts and actions are bent toward evil from childhood. As long as the earth remains, there will be springtime and harvest, cold and heat, winter and summer, day and night." (Genesis 8:20–22)*

Of course, you probably have to take this with a grain of salt, right? I mean, it was God's view about humanity that "all their thoughts were consistently and totally evil" (Genesis 6:5). That's his opinion, not ours.

Maybe God has messed himself up with the impossible standards he created for us. His generosity in promising not to destroy us rings a bit hollow if we're not as bad as he thinks we are. Maybe secretly he realizes he overreacted in the Garden, and now he is making up for it by softening up on the punishment.

But don't forget that one of the key results of eating forbidden fruit was denial—Adam blamed the whole thing on Eve, and Eve blamed it on the serpent. Even today, none of us like to accept the blame for very much of anything.

So either God started out harsh, then eased up when he realized he had overdone his standards, or we're overly blind to our faults, overly blind to the corruption the Bible says was passed down from our first parents.

We have Someone who declares himself our Maker. He says that our first parents were formed to live in his presence but under his ground rules. They made a try at freedom, seeking godhood, and appear to have lost most of the good things they once enjoyed. What is more, some sort of strain of corruption spread to their offspring, so that humanity has every reason to believe it has been condemned and abandoned by its Creator

But—surprise—this same God keeps on leaving his footprints in the mud of our less-than-happy existence, almost as if he were looking for a renewed relationship with us. He is under no illusions that we've improved ourselves. In fact, he sees us more or less totally messed up despite our occasional flashes of goodness. But he is not ready to let go of us.

Either he is wrong about how sorry a lot we are, or he is showing something here that is beyond our imagining—that we really are a mess, but he can't stop loving us.

11

Finding Community, Losing Community

Human beings are compulsive about community. We need one another, crave the presence and comfort of one another, sometimes even to the point of putting ourselves at risk. Recently I watched a TV documentary on college hazing, that time-honored practice of convincing freshman students to do embarrassing or dangerous stunts so they can become part of the accepted crowd. It stressed just how far some students would go to pass their hazing. Every year several of them are badly hurt carrying out whatever action will win them approval. A few die. All of this so that they can be part of the "in" group.

For human beings, the need to be part of community is a central fact of life. Babies at birth are thrust out of the safety of the womb into what must be a terribly hostile world. From the outset, people understand that their dependence on one another goes beyond mere survival into the realm of craving to know they are accepted, loved, valued. Without that reassurance, they simply start fading away. Life becomes sad and frightening without the comfort of others who treasure us.

In this postmodern world, most people are searching for community. Their deepest longing is not to live alone in the middle of a forest or the ocean or the desert, but to find a home in the middle of humanity. People want to belong, need to belong, need to be fed by the encouragement and affirmation of others who are human.

According to Genesis 11, everyone in the beginning lived on the same vast plain. As they grew in numbers, they became worried that something would scatter them, making them vulnerable to extinction.

So they built an enormous tower (such towers were common in the ancient world) with the idea that as long as everyone on the plain could see the tower, they could remain one people. The tower was their identity, a symbol of their unity:

> *At one time the whole world spoke a single language and used the same words. As the people migrated eastward, they found a plain in the land of Babylonia and settled there. They began to talk about construction projects. "Come," they said, "let's make great piles of burnt brick and collect natural asphalt to use as mortar. Let's build a great city with a tower that reaches to the skies—a monument to our greatness! This will bring us together and keep us from scattering all over the world."*
> *(Genesis 11:1–4)*

Not much wrong with this plan, or so it seemed. It makes a lot of sense to me on the surface of things. But God knew that the old temptation to cast him aside and go for independence still plagued humanity. The more populated the plain became, the more confident people would be that they didn't need their Creator and the more they would resist his desire to reach out to them. Once they found themselves completely self-sufficient, that old rebellion of their first parents would take them even further down the road to self-destruction because freedom from God doesn't liberate; according to the Bible, it corrupts. So God took drastic action:

> *But the Lord came down to see the city and the tower the people were building. "Look!" he said. "If they can accomplish this when they have just begun to take advantage of their common language and political unity, just think of what they will do later. Nothing will be impossible for them! Come, let's go down and give them different languages. Then they won't be able to understand each other."*
> *In that way, the Lord scattered them all over the earth; and that ended the building of the city. (Genesis 11:5–8)*

God confused their language. All of a sudden, people could not communicate with their neighbors except within small groups that shared a common tongue. The barriers of language caused people to scatter and start roaming the earth, each language group in search of its own homeland. God did all this, not to mess up their lives, but to make the people he had created in his image more dependent on him.

What does this say about us? Beyond telling us that we are all equally human, so that all people are part of our community, it implies that community in itself won't solve the human problem. While you may feel more secure walking down a dark alley with five of your friends than traveling it alone, there's no guarantee that ten bad guys won't come along and mug the whole lot of you. While you may think you have all the comfort and acceptance you need in the community you call your own, you still have to grapple with the fact that you have to live in this world as an individual, with all the challenges that brings.

The people on the plain who built a tower may not consciously have thought they were using community as a *substitute* for the God they had abandoned, but that was exactly what it amounted to. In their minds, if they could consolidate themselves as a people, they could find the security they needed to live the good life.

How well does human community work? Not too badly when it's going well. Terribly when it's not. But one thing is pretty sure—no matter how much community people make for themselves, they are still individuals. They can still be lonely and afraid, even in a crowd. Community gives us a sense that we are safe, but it offers no guarantees, no permanent solution to the realities that we are still individuals and that no one can protect us from everything.

When God saw the tower going up, he knew that community would be a powerful draw. He also knew that if it were used as a substitute for the relationship with him that he planned when he created them in his image, community would take them even farther from him and would ultimately let them down. It wouldn't satisfy what they were really looking for, something the church father Augustine expressed this way: "Our hearts are restless until they find their rest in You."

That is why he disrupted their society—not to be cruel, but to pull them back from a false substitute for true security, which could only be found in relationship with him. Community is a wonderful thing, but it is no decent replacement for God.

Something is starting to become clear—God, who apparently judged and banished humanity, is still involved with it. True, his remedy seems unusual once again, but it had a purpose to return them to some of the dependence our first parents had before they went on their own and brought misery on themselves.

God can't seem to let go of us. In this lies our hope.

12

The Start of Something Big

You have to think, with all the bad news I've been dropping on you in the preceding chapters, that something had to give eventually. If the Bible is all it's cracked up to be, there has to be a sign of cheer in there somewhere.

Cheer comes in the person of a man named Abram (later Abraham), the father of the Jewish people. He emerged from Mesopotamia and traveled to the territory now known as Israel on the promise of God that great things would happen if he did so.

> *Then the Lord told Abram, "Leave your country, your relatives, and your father's house, and go to the land that I will show you. I will cause you to become the father of a great nation. I will bless you and make you famous, and I will make you a blessing to others. I will bless those who bless you and curse those who curse you. All the families of the earth will be blessed through you." (Genesis 12:1–3)*

We can see one thing right away in this Bible passage—after centuries of relative silence, God was talking to people again. Unless he meant to pass more judgment on them, this was probably a good thing.

So what was the promise he gave? God told Abram he would make him into a great nation and bless him. Abram and his nation, in turn, would bring blessing to the whole world. Blessing? What is that exactly?

It's here that we first catch just how big a deal this event with Abram was. God, having made the world, having watched his highest creation turn away from him, having passed judgment, having purged humanity in a flood, having scattered them at the Tower of Babel when they made another bid for independent power, launched into a plan to "bless" them. Blessing can best be defined as *restoration*. God's pledge was to return Abram and his family to a relationship with him, without judgment, without barriers. A relationship like that of Eden.

Only when you've understood how far down the road of corruption humanity had gone will it make sense what an amazing thing this is—that God, offended and turned off by a humanity that gave up paradise for a failed chance at godhood, should turn around and start a relationship with one of them—Abram—as if the offence had never happened in the first place. Of course, the Bible says it did happen, and Abram was not necessarily a better man than anyone else of his generation. Yet God, who understood full well that Abram himself would likely mess up too, still chose to bless him, to restore him to a relationship with his Maker.

The first part of the blessing smacks of favoritism. God would make Abram's descendents into a great nation, he would bless them, and he would curse anyone who cursed his special chosen family.

But that's not nearly the whole story, because the end of his promise speaks of something bigger, a plan of restoration. "All the families of the earth will be blessed through you" (Genesis 12:3). What does that mean, exactly? I doubt Abram, or even most of his offspring in the next few centuries, knew. Even so, as the promise developed, it became more and more clear that God's blessing on Abram was intended to establish one nation as a showpiece to all the other nations—a people who demonstrated to the world what it would be like to live in utter dependence on God.

The plan God set out was basically pretty simple—create a people committed to him, surround them with divine love and protection (not the security they built for themselves), then draw the other nations of the world back to their Creator by showing the advantages of people living the way he had intended Adam and Eve to live.

This, of course, raises a big question, maybe even a series of them. God had promised to wipe Adam and Eve out if they disobeyed him. But he didn't kill them; he simply let them experience the misery of the consequences their action brought on them. Now he turns around and sets up a plan to bring them back to himself. What kind of a God is this, anyway? Outside of the objections we still have about the negativity of his judgment, he seems to be going back on everything he said.

If he is God, and he is offended by the creatures he made, then lightning bolts should be out and humanity should be toast. Instead, he is working to restore them, to bring them back to Eden. Does this mean that he discovered that we're not as bad as he thought we were? Does it mean he has relaxed his standards now that he sees we can't possibly be as good as he hoped we would be?

Bruce Cockburn, a Canadian singer with a strong social conscience, visited a Guatemalan refugee camp in Mexico in 1983 and heard of the atrocities committed on the common people—brutal, horrible things, like shooting children from attack helicopters. Through tears and a bottle of Bell's, he wrote his now famous song, "If I Had a Rocket Launcher." The lyrics, full of anger, promised to "make somebody pay."

We can understand that kind of anger, even call it "righteous," because injustice and evil that has been done to the innocent cries out for retribution. But God, given the ultimate insult—that his own creation turned on him, defied him, and corrupted itself in every possible way—doesn't get out his rocket launcher and blow them away. He turns around and finds a man to bless with a view to reaching out to the whole world through that one man.

Up to this point, God has been a shadowy figure in many ways, first as the Presence that was there before everything else, then as Creator, then as Judge, then as gracious Walker in the mud of our existence. Now finally, in Abram, we're starting to get a sense of God's heart. He could have destroyed us. There could have been no you, no me. But for some unaccountable reason, he reached out to a man named Abram and gave him a promise—"All the families of the earth will be blessed through you." In this lies our first sparkle of hope, since God put the curse on the serpent in the Garden of Eden.

13

A Promise Like You've Never Seen

Abram soon realized that his big dream, given to him by the Creator himself, was in trouble. Though God had promised to make him into a great nation, Abram had no territory to call his own, because the Promised Land was occupied by others and he was getting old. So was his wife. The hope of having children was fading, and without children and land, nationhood was doomed.

This shadowy, elusive God we've been observing was the first to notice Abram's despair. We read:

> *After this, the word of the Lord came to Abram in a vision:*
> *"Do not be afraid, Abram. I am your shield,*
> *your very great reward." (Genesis 15:1 NIV)*

I don't know about you, but having the Almighty come down and tell me something like that would be a big deal. I mean, here I am—the creature who should be dead—but God promises to be my protector, my very great reward. He tells me not to be afraid.

Fear is something that lurks in all of us. No matter how old we get, we repeatedly find ourselves in dark and haunted places, hungering for some perfect parent to move alongside us and tell us, "Don't be afraid. I am your protector." Surprisingly, Abram wasn't entirely impressed by God's kind words:

> *But Abram replied, "O Sovereign Lord, what good are all your blessings when I don't even have a son? Since I don't have a son, Eliezer of Damascus, a servant in my household, will inherit all my wealth. You have given me no children, so one of my servants will have to be my heir." (Genesis 15:2–3)*

All he wanted was some assurance that God's original promise could happen, some evidence that the impossible was still possible. Notice how much, in the Bible's view of things, Abram's meaning was tied up with God's presence and power in his life. God had told Abram amazing things, not only about the promise of nationhood but about the Creator's love for a creature who no more deserved blessing than any other member of the fallen. And now that Abram was bound to him, God didn't seem to be following through.

There's the problem. We humans don't do at all well muddling along on our own, but at least when we're our own persons, we have some control over our destiny. Sure, life is the way it is, full of pain and struggle. Certainly we long for more. But we resist losing control of our futures and becoming dependent on some Higher Power, let alone being a slave to one. If we were to cast our lot in with God, we know we would lose our independence. God could then take his own sweet time meeting our needs, and we would be as pathetic as Abram, saying, "You promised me . . ."

But let's hold judgment on that thought for a minute:

> *Then the Lord told him, "Bring me a three-year-old heifer, a three-year-old female goat, a three-year-old ram, a turtledove, and a young pigeon." Abram took all these and killed them. He cut each one down the middle and laid the halves side by side. He did not, however, divide the birds in half. Some vultures came down to eat the carcasses, but Abram chased them away. That evening, as the sun was going down, Abram fell into a deep sleep. He saw a terrifying vision of darkness and horror. (Genesis 15:9–12)*

Abram cut several animals in two and arranged the halves opposite each other in two rows with a corridor in the middle. After that, he stayed awake guarding the carcasses until a thick and terrible darkness drove him into sleep.

> *Then the Lord told Abram, "You can be sure that your descendants will be strangers in a foreign land, and they will be oppressed as slaves for four hundred years. But I will punish the nation that enslaves them, and in the end they will come away with great wealth." (Genesis 15:13–14)*

So Abram would actually have a family, and his descendents would receive the promise, but they would have to wait four hundred years for it. The renewed promise God made wasn't without its problems: Four centuries of servitude would pass before the nation could emerge. As the story later unfolded, Abram's children actually needed all four hundred of those years to become what God intended them to be. But the heart of the promise was there in Abram's time, affirmed by God himself.

What, then, does this have to do with the animal carcasses arranged in rows?

> *As the sun went down and it became dark, Abram saw a smoking firepot and a flaming torch pass between the halves of the carcasses. So the Lord made a covenant with Abram that day and said, "I have given this land to your descendants, all the way from the border of Egypt to the great Euphrates River—the land of the Kenites, Kenizzites, Kadmonites, Hittites, Perizzites, Rephaites, Amorites, Canaanites, Girgashites, and Jebusites." (Genesis 15:17–21)*

Now it probably makes even less sense, so let me hasten to explain. In the ancient world there was lots of conflict, tons of distrust. When various groups of people made promises to each other, they tended to want to seal the whole thing with a solemn oath by means of a formal covenant, a legal agreement. To cut up some animals and walk between the pieces was a way for each of the partners in such an agreement to swear an oath along the lines of, "May what happened to these animals happen to me if I ever go back on what I've promised."

In the account we're looking at, the presence of God in the form of a blazing torch passed between the pieces as God promised to give Abram a vast tract of land owned by other nations. The Creator was in essence saying, "I promise this on my very existence. If I fail to give it to you, may I be as dead as the heifer and the goat."

It worked like this—if God was going to call Abram and his

descendents into a relationship with him that required utter dependence on him for their future, he was going to make unbreakable promises to them in return. There wasn't going to be a risk to this thing. Abram's timing might not coincide with God's timing—a four-hundred-year delay seldom does—but God would make sure that everything was fulfilled and Abram ended up on the side of mega blessing.

Let's go back a bit to one part of the chapter we left out: "And Abram believed the Lord, and the Lord declared him righteous because of his faith" (Genesis 15:6). You, no doubt, understand that Abram believed the promise, soon to be guaranteed by God's solemn oath. But what does it mean to be declared righteous (*righteous* here meaning nothing less than having the slate wiped clean)?

Abram was no better than the rest of humanity—he had acted selfishly, too, just like all of us. He had earned himself a pack of judgment. He had chalked up for himself a sentence of death, just like Adam and Eve, his first parents. Yet God had looked beyond all that in setting him up as the founder of a new plan to bless the world. And now, simply because Abram believed him, God gave Abram a credit—like wiping out a bad debt and canceling the barrier between them. No more penalty, nothing stopping him from recovering his relationship with the One who made him.

Bottom line, Abram at one point had been his own man, setting his own destiny, just like the rest of us. Along came God, who said, "I have a plan for you." Abram, despite many doubts and fears, abandoned his independence and turned his destiny over to God. God, in turn, made promises that could not be broken.

Scary stuff, isn't it? If your definition of what it is to be human is built around your power to be your own person, to plan, to do, to be what you determine, then you're going to be shaken by Abram's bargain. He gave everything up to commit himself to God and God's promise.

But let's remember that the Bible gives a different perspective on being human. According to the Bible, being your own person makes you less than what you could be, not more. According to the Bible, finding your own destiny in your own way means walking away from what you were created for.

Bad bargain or good bargain? The Bible claims it was the only intelligent choice a man could make. You may well have some reservations, because giving up our personal independence is something our heritage tells us never to do.

Was Abram a fool or a man of wisdom? You tell me.

14

Walking with the One Who Made Him

I didn't mention earlier that Abram was seventy-five years old when he left his city of Haran to go to the land that God planned to give him. A whole lot of trust was going on here—from Abram because he was too old for such an adventure, and from God because he must have known that Abram was too old for such an adventure. The key factor was that Abram was willing to go.

This is not to say that there weren't bumps in the journey. Abram came to what is now Israel and Palestine with no land to call his own. For many years he wandered as a nomad.

Once, when famine hit, he and his wife Sarah went down to Egypt, where Sarah, a beautiful woman though elderly, was spotted by the ruling Pharaoh. Marriage bonds were considered sacred in the ancient world, so if a king wanted someone's wife, he would generally have to kill the husband to break the marriage "legitimately." Abram, fearing for his life, told Pharaoh that Sarah was his sister. If God hadn't intervened by inflicting serious diseases on Pharaoh and his household, Sarah could have been lost to Abram forever (Genesis 12:10–20).

The Creator would have had good cause for abandoning such an unfaithful person, but God hung onto him. In future years, Abram ran into tons of conflict with his greedy nephew Lot, even having to go to war to rescue him at one point, but God's man began showing his character in the positive choices he made (Genesis 13–14). What was God up to during all this? Simply getting ready to make a covenant with Abram (Genesis 15), guaranteeing that all the promises would be fulfilled.

One day, fifteen years after the first promise, a "messenger" from God showed up and told Abram, now renamed Abraham, "About this time next year I will return, and your wife Sarah will have a son" (Genesis 18:10). Sarah was listening nearby and laughed out of sheer disbelief. But Abraham seems to have believed the promise, even though he was now ancient.

This couple soon found themselves in the Negev region where Sarah, old as she was, ended up being hit on again by the local ruler. Abraham, believe it or not, did the "she's-my-sister" routine once more and once more almost lost the woman who was supposed to be the mother of his child (Genesis 20).

There's a pattern here—God reaches out, Abraham trusts for awhile, Abraham drops the ball; God rescues him, God renews the promise, Abraham trusts for awhile, drops the ball; God rescues . . . and so on. You would think the Creator could have chosen a better person than Abraham to carry out his plan of reaching the world. Or at least he should have terminated the relationship when Abraham proved unreliable.

Back to the promise God had made—within the year, as predicted, Sarah did give birth to a son they named Isaac, a miracle baby because his mother was far too old to be bearing children (Genesis 21). The boy grew up well—healthy and intelligent—but God had a plan for Abraham that would rock him to the core. When Isaac was in his teens, God one day told Abraham to take his only son into the hills and offer him as a sacrifice, killing him on an altar of stone.

What? What kind of God is this? First he promises Abraham a son to fulfill the promise of turning Abraham into a great nation, then he says, "Take him out and kill him." The logic of it escapes me, and the brutality of this command (delivered to a man and his son who have made themselves vulnerable by committing themselves to God) is almost unthinkable.

To begin to grasp what is going on in the mind of God here, we have to understand that he is in the business of transforming his fallen creation. Abraham had long shown a rocky track record—sometimes trusting and trustworthy, sometimes doing whatever it took to save his life or achieve his goals. Something more was needed to bring him around and make him the man God needed him to be.

This isn't really all that unusual. The Bible shows a consistent pattern of God choosing people who are not full of themselves, people with flaws, people like us; then he transforms them. Let me give you a few examples:

There was Gideon, a farmer with no military experience, who defeated a vast army with three hundred men (Judges 6); David, a shepherd, who became Israel's greatest king, committed a murder, which resulted years later in his own son stealing his throne, only to be restored to his throne by a forgiving God (1 and 2 Samuel); Peter, a fisherman, who abandoned Jesus when he was crucified but went on to become a significant leader in the early church (Luke 22:54–62; Acts 2).

If all I had to tell you about the meaning of life was that we started perfect then chose our own path of destruction, there wouldn't be much point. The Bible says that there is Someone from outside who formed us, watched us mess up our lives, then, in spite of everything, picked us up and transformed us.

So Abraham, having no clue what God was up to, trusted him, brought his only son into the wilderness, prepared an alter, convinced the boy to lie on it, and raised a knife to drive it into Isaac's chest. At the very last second, a voice shouted from heaven, "Stop! Don't lay a hand on the boy." It was God calling a halt to the whole thing. Nearby a ram had been caught in a thicket. Abraham offered the ram instead of his son (Genesis 22:1–19).

It seems like a barbaric event all around, but evidently God had a purpose in telling Abraham to sacrifice his son, then calling it off at the last second. His purpose? Simply to bring Abraham at last to a place of utter trust in him. Why? Because to live out a promise like the one God had made, Abraham needed to learn utter trust, the kind of trust that goes on trusting even when God appears to make no sense.

In response to his new faith, Abraham bought a field when Sarah later died (Genesis 23). Besides showing the extent of Abraham's newfound faith, the story of the buying of the field is itself a fascinating example of ancient barter. Abraham asked the Hittites for a certain field with a cave in it. They offered to give it to him so they could take it back whenever they wanted, but he knew this would not provide him full title, so he offered to buy it. The Hittites didn't want to sell him the land, so they asked for an enormously large sum, thinking that Abraham would just walk away from the deal. Abraham paid the amount without blinking.

What's the point? Just that, with utter trust in God, Abraham invested in the land he had been promised and got full title to a piece of it. Later, while his descendents suffered in Egypt, they would remember and gain strength from the one piece of property they owned in God's land of promise.

Abraham could have ignored the call of God and gone his own way, been his own man, found his own freedom. But it didn't diminish him to choose the dangerous path of absolute trust in a Creator with a plan; it made him stronger, more alive. It didn't enslave him; it made him free to become much more than he could have been on his own.

And in spite of Abraham's weakness, his failures, his rebellion, God kept on coming back to restore the relationship. We find a fitting epitaph later in the Bible:

> *It was by faith that Abraham obeyed when God called him to leave home and go to another land that God would give him as his inheritance. He went without knowing where he was going. And even when he reached the land God promised him, he lived there by faith—for he was like a foreigner, living in a tent. And so did Isaac and Jacob, to whom God gave the same promise. Abraham did this because he was confidently looking forward to a city with eternal foundations, a city designed and built by God. It was by faith that Sarah together with Abraham was able to have a child, even though they were too old and Sarah was barren. Abraham believed that God would keep his promise. And so a whole nation came from this one man, Abraham, who was too old to have any children—a nation with so many people that, like the stars of the sky and the sand on the seashore, there is no way to count them. (Hebrews 11:8–12)*

What am I telling you about Abraham? Beyond the fact that he is still highly honored in three religions, the fact is that we all need a story to make sense of all the strange fragments of our lives. I'm offering you a story. Sure it's someone else's, but other people's stories can become our own if we make sense of them. Over the next few chapters I'm going to give you a number of other people's stories. Maybe some of them will strike a familiar chord with yours, and you will find yourself echoing their experiences.

If our meaning is bound up with God, the best way to understand that meaning is to walk with people who walked with God. Maybe they were crazy, but, then again, maybe they discovered something the rest of us have missed

15

Pharaoh Was Mistaken

As predicted in Genesis 15, Abraham had a son, and that son had a son who became Israel, the father of the Israelites. As predicted, they moved to Egypt to escape a famine and stayed there four hundred years.

Some people see these four centuries as evidence that the Israelites had a profound lack of trust in the promise of God, but their stay in Egypt actually fulfilled a couple of important purposes. First, because the ancient Egyptians were racists, Israel as a people was allowed to develop and flourish in its own territory within Egypt, separated from the true citizens of this nation. Second, their stay presented a great opportunity for God to do something big.

In this book we've been seeking the meaning of life, the purpose for everything. But we know that it's tough enough to figure out who we are, let alone understand the events that shape us and then try to make sense of our place in the world. We've seen the first couple decide that their place was out there on their own, out from under the control of God. The result was disastrous for them, leading us to believe they never were equipped by their Maker to be able to sustain life outside of the boundaries God set for it.

We've seen Abraham, who threw in his lot with God despite the rocky road he ended up traveling. Did he settle for second best? Maybe he missed a chance to build his own empire. Maybe he missed the opportunity to plan his own life.

In spite of our possible doubts about the wisdom of his decision, it appears that the life he was given in return wasn't too shabby at all, thank you very much. In the end, he had a much bigger empire than he could have won for himself on his own.

Yet now, after four hundred years, his people were in trouble, and the promise of inheriting the land was getting as dim as a cheap flash-light in a heavy fog. The Egyptians had left them alone at first, but eventually heavier hands had come into the picture, and Israel became a slave nation for Egypt's aggressive construction program. The Israelites were doomed to stay there in a foreign land and never achieve their dream unless someone much stronger intervened.

It's quite a story—how an unfeeling pharaoh, worried by Israel's population growth, tried to have all Israelite baby boys killed. How one mother left her infant son Moses to be found by the pharaoh's daughter, who raised him as her own child. How the adult Moses saw a fellow Israelite being beaten and killed the Egyptian doing the beating. How Moses fled and lived out in the wilderness for forty years until one day he encountered a bush on fire . . .

> *One day Moses was tending the flock of his father-in-law,*
> *Jethro, the priest of Midian, and he went deep into the*
> *wilderness near Sinai, the mountain of God. Suddenly, the*
> *angel of the Lord appeared to him as a blazing fire in a bush.*
> *Moses was amazed because the bush was engulfed in flames, but*
> *it didn't burn up. "Amazing!" Moses said to himself. "Why*
> *isn't that bush burning up? I must go over to see this."*
> *(Exodus 3:1–3)*

A bush on fire that wouldn't burn up was quite a draw to a curious observer. Moses went closer, and out of the bush came a voice. Up to this point, Moses had been pretty much making his own destiny, though his life in the desert was a whole lot shabbier than it had been in the palace of the pharaoh. Now, things were about to take a strange turn. The voice, who declared himself to be God, spoke:

> *Then the Lord told him, "You can be sure I have seen the misery*
> *of my people in Egypt. I have heard their cries for deliverance*
> *from their harsh slave drivers. Yes, I am aware of their suffering.*
> *So I have come to rescue them from the Egyptians and lead them*
> *out of Egypt into their own good and spacious land. It is a land*
> *flowing with milk and honey—the land where the Canaanites,*
> *Hittites, Amorites, Perizzites, Hivites, and Jebusites live. The*
> *cries of the people of Israel have reached me, and I have seen*
> *how the Egyptians have oppressed them with heavy tasks. Now*

> *go, for I am sending you to Pharaoh. You will lead my people,*
> *the Israelites, out of Egypt." (Exodus 3:7–10)*

Once again, God took a man out of the blue and said, "I want you to do a job for me." But this wasn't some nasty divine scheme to make Moses a slave for selfish purposes. The cry of the oppressed Israelites had reached the consciousness of God, and he was determined to rescue them. True, since he is Almighty God, he could have done it himself through some miracle or other, but instead he chose a man to lead the charge.

Moses didn't want the job. He couldn't see himself as a leader, which is probably exactly why God chose him. There is a consistent pattern in the Bible of God choosing ordinary Joes or Janes when he wants great things done, because ordinary people are much more likely to put themselves completely in God's hands. Despite Moses' objections, God insisted, and the future leader of the Israelites agreed.

Moses, with his brother Aaron as his spokesman, went to the pharaoh to ask that the enslaved children of Israel be allowed to return to the land God had promised them. Pharaoh, a real beauty with a heart of granite, said "no." Moses performed some miracles with God's help, and Pharaoh declared himself unimpressed. This was your classic no-win situation—Moses with no personal power demanding the impossible from a ruler with all the power.

Imagine that you've just thrown the perfect party and invited people you thought would be the perfect guests. But after they had a few drinks in them, your guests turned into louts—double-dipping the chips, messing up the sandwiches on the food bar, dunking their heads in the punch bowl, doing terrible things to the carpet like a bunch of barbarians. You invited them; you went to all the work to make everything perfect; and they threw it all in your face.

That's where God was with someone like Pharaoh. We're far from the Garden of Eden now, in a place where no one recognizes God's people anymore, and the ruler doesn't care a fig for the One who created the world. "You say God has a plan?" his actions retort. "Well, who's God and why should I care? You tell me he's the one who threw this party? That means nothing to me. Let me just dunk my head in this punch bowl."

But according to the biblical account, things were not what they seemed. Pharaoh had gravely underestimated his opponent—not Moses, but the God Moses trusted. Almost immediately, bad things began to happen. The River Nile filled with blood and stank to high heaven. Then the land became infested in turn with frogs, gnats, and flies. The livestock died of some strange disease, and the Egyptians were afflicted with infectious boils. Still Pharaoh refused to give in to Moses' demand. Hailstorms, locusts, and constant darkness followed. Finally, when all else had failed, God struck the firstborn of the land— people and animals—stone-cold dead. Only then did Pharaoh give the order for the Israelites to be released.

We have something here to reckon with. The fact is that God, though he normally doesn't, can ruin your whole day. People cross him regularly, all of us, ignoring his claim that he made us and can determine our destiny. But when he wants to, according to the Bible, he can conquer all resistance and bring us to the end of our rebellion.

That may seem like a nasty reality, and we can be grateful that he seldom exercises his option, but make no mistake—he holds our future in his hands. He can bless us or snuff us. The fact that he can dominate us, of course, does not mean that he will as a matter of course. But the God of the Bible, the God who claims to have made you, is someone to take absolutely seriously.

In fact, as part of the explanation for inflicting the plagues on the Egyptians, God said, "When I show the Egyptians my power and force them to let the Israelites go, they will realize that I am the Lord" (Exodus 7:5). His intention was to make Egypt know who was Lord, Boss, Supreme Being-in-Charge.

What does this have to do with the meaning of life? Just this—we go blithely along, claiming that we are independent, the masters of our fate and captains of our souls. We value our power to control our personal situation and make our own decisions. All the while, the One who created us is standing by with the power to turn our lives on their heads, to bless us or to end us. If this is true, any notion of ignoring him comes with the reality that he is not ignoring us. We are not the independent creatures we think we are.

Pharaoh thought he was absolutely secure in defying puny Moses. He was wrong. Before God was done with him, the absolute ruler of Egypt was begging the Israelites to leave.

16

Finding Home

From the very first day in each of our lives, let's admit it, we've resisted being dominated by anyone. Adam and Eve's story is our story. We want to be free, independent, masters of our own destiny. No chains on us, no nagging voice in our ears demanding, "Do what I tell you." But we've discovered that the first couple lost a good thing by striking out on their own. Was their "freedom" worth it?

Let me share something that's been lurking in everything we've looked at so far. It's simply this—according to the Bible, we were not made to be successful at independence, because God made us to be his, under his care and direction. Our true home, our true identity, is where God is.

The stories of humanity's many failures to get life right are as obvious as the TV news. In the Bible, God often pointed out the problem of human inability to find the good life. One of the more realistic visions of human life is the book of Ecclesiastes. Here's a taste:

> *Again I observed all the oppression that takes place in our*
> *world. I saw the tears of the oppressed, with no one to comfort*
> *them. The oppressors have great power, and the victims are*
> *helpless. So I concluded that the dead are better off than the*
> *living. And most fortunate of all are those who were never born.*
> *For they have never seen all the evil that is done in our world.*
> *Then I observed that most people are motivated to success by*
> *their envy of their neighbors. But this, too, is meaningless, like*
> *chasing the wind. (Ecclesiastes 4:1–4)*

A man might have a hundred children and live to be very old.
But if he finds no satisfaction in life and in the end does not
even get a decent burial, I say he would have been better off
born dead. I realize that his birth would have been meaningless
and ended in darkness. He wouldn't even have had a name, and
he would never have seen the sun or known of its existence. Yet
he would have had more peace than he has in growing up to be
an unhappy man. He might live a thousand years twice over but
not find contentment. And since he must die like everyone
else—well, what's the use?
All people spend their lives scratching for food, but they never
seem to have enough. Considering this, do wise people really
have any advantage over fools? Do poor people gain anything
by being wise and knowing how to act in front of others?
(Ecclesiastes 6:3–8)

Tragic words indeed, but they ring true. The writer of this book of the Bible had seen the world of human independence from God's eyes, and it wasn't pretty.

Now we come to the hard part—the Bible makes it plain that our true identity is found in abandoning independence and becoming utterly dependent on the One who made us. Independence is something we can only do badly because we were never equipped for it.

This is a bitter pill because it flies in the face of everything we've been taught about what it means to be human. We grew up believing that we're supposed to forge our own futures and that the greatest evil is to be dominated by someone else. Now we hear that Someone has a claim on us because he is responsible for our very existence. And, what is more, the same Someone tells us that he never made us for independent life because we were constructed only to operate successfully under his control.

You don't have to absorb this all at once. Give it time to percolate in your consciousness. In the meantime, come with me into the desert for awhile. Deep in the Sinai, we find Israel trekking across the burning sand toward their Promised Land. Behind them, they've left Egypt in shambles. Ahead of them is an impossible horror of blazing sun with no food or water, not to mention fierce tribes determined to wipe them out.

They came to Mount Sinai, and God told them to wait there while Moses climbed the slope to receive a message from their Maker. The document he was given on tablets of stone is familiar. It has come down to us as the Ten Commandments, part of God's covenant with his people that spelled out the relationship he expected to have with them. The fact that it came in the form of law and regulation makes it clear that God didn't expect these people he had chosen to consider themselves his equals like the serpent had promised them in the Garden of Eden. He expected to be in charge.

Let's look at the commandments he delivered to Israel and see what possible value they could have had for humanity. The first of them called for an exclusive relationship with God. We read:

Then God instructed the people as follows:

> *"I am the Lord your God, who rescued you*
> *from slavery in Egypt.*
> *Do not worship any other gods besides me."*
> *(Exodus 20:1–3)*

There it is, that exclusive claim on our lives. It's built here on an assumption that is a real shocker—that we are not utterly free of all enslavement, but we simply choose the gods that will control us. The Bible is saying that someone or something is going to dominate the direction of our lives no matter what we try to do about it. The important thing is to choose the right ruler.

Could this be true? The fact is that most of us find it a struggle to discover our identity and rise above our circumstances, even above our own personalities. Could it be that we're governed by forces beyond our control? We talk about Fate as if it were a god, a fickle one that smacks us down just when we're getting somewhere. Then, of course, there's the old call of the serpent—"Live for yourself and you will be like God"—except that the minute we try it, we fall into a dismal world of failure and interpersonal conflict.

The second commandment is the other side of the coin from the first:

> *Do not make idols of any kind, whether in the shape of birds or*
> *animals or fish. You must never worship or bow down to them,*
> *for I, the Lord your God, am a jealous God who will not share*
> *your affection with any other god! (Exodus 20:4–5)*

No idols allowed, no worship of other gods. Why? Because God is jealous, though probably not in the way that we measure jealousy as selfishness. It stands to reason that someone who said, "You shall have no other gods," would also make it clear that his people were not supposed to worship anyone but him.

This demand for an exclusive relationship could sound pretty self-serving. We've all seen jealousy in clinging relationships that make slaves of people. But let's look at it a different way. If you formed humanity in your image, then watched your creation walk away into chaos, wouldn't you want to bring them back, assuming you had gotten past wanting to destroy them utterly? We could accuse God of being the spurned lover who doesn't know when to back off, but the alternative is that he knows something we don't—that there is no joy in other gods—and he simply wants to restore to us what we've lost.

God, according to the Bible, wants all humanity to understand that he is indeed God. We are supposed to worship him rather than treating him like a joke or an object of contempt. So the third command reinforces the first two:

> *Do not misuse the name of the Lord your God.*
> *The Lord will not let you go unpunished if you misuse his*
> *name. (Exodus 20:7)*

In the beginning, he was Creator, and life in the Garden worked—it really did. Then the first humans defied him. His name—his character—took a hit that it has been taking ever since. That is why God's people had to remember that disrespecting his name didn't fit the pattern of being God's people. It fits the pattern of rebels.

To help them remember the special day they were created, God dedicated one day in the week for rest and reflection, not a bad idea even now:

> *Remember to observe the Sabbath day by keeping it holy. Six*
> *days a week are set apart for your daily duties and regular work,*
> *but the seventh day is a day of rest dedicated to the Lord your*
> *God. On that day no one in your household may do any kind of*
> *work. This includes you, your sons and daughters, your male*
> *and female servants, your livestock, and any foreigners living*
> *among you. For in six days the Lord made the heavens, the*
> *earth, the sea, and everything in them; then he rested on the*
> *seventh day. That is why the Lord blessed the Sabbath day and*
> *set it apart as holy. (Exodus 20:8–11)*

Once a week, God's people were given the opportunity to recall their roots, to keep from forgetting that they did not make themselves. That was worth something to their relationship with the Creator.

The next few commandments come in rapid fire order. Each one was intended to help human beings to live humanly, the way they were made to live in the Garden:

> *Honor your father and mother. Then you will live a long, full life in the land the Lord your God will give you.*
> *Do not murder.*
> *Do not commit adultery.*
> *Do not steal.*
> *Do not testify falsely against your neighbor.*
> *Do not covet your neighbor's house. Do not covet your neighbor's wife, male or female servant, ox or donkey, or anything else your neighbor owns. (Exodus 20:12–17)*

Do you see what we have here? These commands were not some terrible burden. They were restoration. God was reaching out to the Israelites to tell them that people related to him, people who have abandoned their rebellion and want to come back, need to relearn how to live. Humanity had been out of the Garden for a long time. To be restored, they needed to grasp the ground rules that made life in the Garden worth living.

But let's get rid of the notion that, by following the rules, they could earn a relationship with God. That was never the intention. God had already chosen them and made promises to them. What he wanted in return was a simple commitment from them that they were ready to abandon their rebellion. Thus, he called them to a solemn oath.

We read in Exodus 19 that Moses, and Moses alone, was called into the presence of God to hear the law dictated to him. The first version of the Ten Commandments managed to get itself destroyed, and Moses had to get another copy from God.

When he finally had the stone tablets in a form he could use, Moses took the law and recited it to the people. The next part is gory—young bulls were sacrificed, and half of the collected blood was sprinkled on an altar before God. The rest was saved.

Gathering the people again, Moses gave them a final reading of God's law. They in turn responded with the words, "We will do everything the Lord has told us to do" (Exodus 24:3). In other words, "We will obey." At that moment we read:

> *Then Moses sprinkled the blood from the basins over the people and said, "This blood confirms the covenant the Lord has made with you in giving you these laws." (Exodus 24:8)*

Blood everywhere. A little extreme, don't you think? As near as Bible scholars can figure out, the blood sprinkled on all the people that sealed their oath meant something like, "May what happened to those bulls happen to us if we should ever rebel against God again."

But these people weren't whipped puppies battered by their Maker into submission and slavery. They knew exactly what they were doing there in the desert below Mount Sinai, and they chose it intentionally.

Why? Because they had seen God rescue them from slavery by conquering an evil king. They had seen him provide for them despite their grumbling. They had seen the truth—that they weren't very good at living apart from him, and he was offering them a way to find their meaning. With their commitment, they were starting a long and hard journey, not just into the wilderness, but ultimately back to the Garden. The laws weren't there to burden them but to teach them how to live.

God was on his way, with one people in one place, to restoring what Adam and Eve abandoned. The people he made were heading for home.

17

Not a Good Story if You Eat at Burger King

As God's people traveled through the wilderness toward the land promised four hundred years before to Abraham, the Lord told them to build a tabernacle, a portable temple that would serve as the place where the high priest maintained Israel's relationship with the One who led them. But this was no mere shrine. It was also a place where gory ceremonies were performed to deal with a nagging problem—that even people who have pledged to obey their Maker end up doing it less than perfectly.

You see, God declares himself to be "holy," a technical term meaning that he is utterly pure, utterly different from fallen human beings, though we share his image. Every act of rebellion among his people was an offense to him, creating a horrible barrier between a perfect God and contaminated humans. You can scoff at the notion that we offend a holy God simply by stepping out of line once in awhile, but the Bible makes it plain that he is, indeed, offended.

Moses, while leading the Israelites toward the Promised Land, told them: "Remember *how angry* you made the Lord your God out in the wilderness. From the day you left Egypt until now, you have constantly rebelled against him" (Deuteronomy 9:7, emphasis added). King David, ruler of Israel, once wrote: "Point out anything in me that offends you, and lead me along the path of everlasting life" (Psalm 139:24). The early Christian leader, Paul the apostle, wrote: "The day will surely come when God, by Jesus Christ, will judge everyone's secret life" (Romans 2:16). All of this tells us that it is indeed possible to offend God.

So what could be done to avoid judgment? The Israelites had promised to walk with their God and trust him to lead them to the land of promise, but they were constantly alienating themselves from him through their own weakness and selfishness, just like we would have done in their place. Well, God proposed a solution, but it wasn't an easy one.

> *The Lord said to Moses, "Warn your brother Aaron not to enter*
> *the Most Holy Place behind the inner curtain whenever he*
> *chooses; the penalty for intrusion is death. For the Ark's cover—*
> *the place of atonement—is there, and I myself am present in the*
> *cloud over the atonement cover.*
> *When Aaron enters the sanctuary area, he must follow*
> *these instructions fully. He must first bring a young*
> *bull for a sin offering and a ram for a whole burnt offering."*
> *(Leviticus 16:2–3)*

We have some technical language here. The word *atonement* shouldn't scare you—it simply means "something that is done to turn away the anger of God." So God is angry? Yes, I'm afraid so. According to the Bible, he made a perfect world, and we turned around and spat in his face. But he's not angry like we're angry, which usually leads to making somebody pay. He's angry all right, but instead of immediately lashing out, he makes a way to have his anger diverted.

It takes something nasty, though, to deflect the anger of God. Aaron, the high priest, was told to slaughter a young bull and a ram. Blood flowed everywhere, lots of it. And this was only just the sacrifice for the priest to cleanse himself so he would be fit to enter into the presence of God to offer further sacrifice for the people of Israel.

I can imagine what all this sounds like to you. Ancient barbarism is one thing, but we live in a different world, and the idea of an angry God appeased by blood just doesn't fly anymore. But look at it this way—if the people you made had turned on you and embraced a life that wounded you deeply; if you knew you could snuff them and be done with humanity; if you wanted them back instead but knew they had to understand what their rebellion had cost them and you—would the blood sacrifice of a substitute be shocking enough to do the trick?

The instructions went on:

> *"Then he must bring the two male goats and present them to the Lord at the entrance of the Tabernacle. He is to cast sacred lots to determine which goat will be sacrificed to the Lord and which one will be the scapegoat. The goat chosen to be sacrificed to the Lord will be presented by Aaron as a sin offering. The goat chosen to be the scapegoat will be presented to the Lord alive. When it is sent away into the wilderness, it will make atonement for the people." (Leviticus 16:7–10)*

Aaron was to take two goats and choose them by lot for two destinies. One would be slaughtered—more blood—and the other, the scapegoat, would have all the evil and rebellion of the people recited over it. Then it would be sent alive into the desert as a symbol that the evil had left the camp.

You may be saying to yourself that these sacrifices shouldn't need to involve actual blood (which is both violent and gross), but the command to Aaron about what to do with the sacrificed animals makes it plain that blood was central to the whole thing:

> *"Then he must dip his finger into the blood of the bull and sprinkle it on the front of the atonement cover and then seven times against the front of the Ark.*
> *"Then Aaron must slaughter the goat as a sin offering for the people and bring its blood behind the inner curtain. There he will sprinkle the blood on the atonement cover and against the front of the Ark, just as he did with the bull's blood." (Leviticus 16:14–15)*

It was bad enough performing these sickening events once, but they were actually repeated once a year, for centuries. And all of it was commanded by God.

The biggest challenge for us is to figure out what it meant, this Day of Atonement that arrived like clockwork every fall. Let's first of all understand why blood had to be shed. It doesn't make sense that people who depended on their animals for survival would so easily cut their throats and offer their carcasses to God.

The clue to the meaning of blood comes from a commandment related to food laws in the next chapter. Israel was told to drain the blood from animals they killed for food and not to consume blood like some sort of table condiment. Why not? Because it was not for common use. It had a special purpose.

> *And I will turn against anyone, whether an Israelite or a foreigner living among you, who eats or drinks blood in any form. I will cut off such a person from the community, for the life of any creature is in its blood. I have given you the blood so you can make atonement for your sins. It is the blood, representing life, that brings you atonement. That is why I said to the Israelites: "You and the foreigners who live among you must never eat or drink blood." (Leviticus 17:10–12)*

The value of blood to this "atonement," this turning away of the anger of God, lay in the fact that "the life of a creature is in its blood." This is true, actually. You take any animal or human and drain its blood, and what happens? It dies. Blood is the elixir of life that flows through us. To shed blood is to kill. What God was saying was, "In order for your rebellion to be taken care of, so I can forgive you and nurture you, something has to die." The animals that shed their blood were a substitute for the people of Israel who got to live.

This brutal annual ceremony still raises problems. It stands to reason that God should simply be able to forgive. If, as the Bible says, all of us have walked away from him, have offended him, have messed up his plan and our lives in the bargain—if all of that is true, we should be able to go to him and say, "We're very, very sorry," and he should respond, "That's all right. Why don't we start again with a fresh slate?"

Instead, for Israel, God made forgiveness a difficult and bloody procedure. Why? The answer from God's perspective is quite simple. He told Adam and Eve that in the day they ate the forbidden fruit, they would die. And in a sense, they did. They created a gulf between themselves and their Creator, according to the Bible. If God is the source of all life, being cut off from him must amount, at least, to a living death. Simply saying we're sorry isn't enough.

A later prophet of God put it well with these words:

> *Listen! The Lord is not too weak to save you, and he is not becoming deaf. He can hear you when you call. But there is a problem—your sins have cut you off from God. Because of your sin, he has turned away and will not listen anymore. (Isaiah 59:1–2)*

Look at it from God's perspective. How easy is it for any one of us to say we're sorry if we find ourselves in big trouble? But do we mean it? Do we even understand what we've done to cause the offense in the first place? The enormity of an Adam or an Eve rising up against the Holy One who made them is something none of us can grasp fully. It's a spit in the face, an upraised middle finger, and more. Thus God determined that simply offering us easy forgiveness would teach us nothing about the enormity of what we've done in our bid for independence. Forgiveness had to come hard.

God's people had to see the blood to understand that when you strike out on your own without your Maker, the only way to get back home is to have something die—either you or a substitute for you. When the Israelites saw the blood flow every Day of Atonement, they understood once again that the price for independence is too high to be paid with cheap forgiveness. Though they didn't know it at the time, this Day was also a preview of the crucifixion of Jesus, who was to arrive on the scene centuries later.

The sacrifices had to be repeated because every year, Israel, like us, forgot that they were made to be God's people, and they lived as if they were their own people. Even when they tried really hard to recapture the relationship of the Garden, they failed at it, not because they were weaker than most other folks, but simply because they were exactly the same as most other folks.

We live in a Burger King world in which what we eat is sanitized and what we experience is far from the reality of a day devoted to blood sacrifice. In many ways, that's a shame. At least Israel, once a year, had the opportunity to see themselves the way their Maker saw them. The picture wasn't pretty. The only compensation was that they came out of this bloody day forgiven.

18

Winning with the Odds Against You

Israel fled Egypt, offered sacrifices to God in the desert, faltered, wandered far too long in the wilderness, and eventually claimed the Promised Land that had been pledged to Abraham over four hundred years before. But, contrary to the command from God, the Israelites didn't remove all of the previous inhabitants from the land, and in the next few centuries those inhabitants would become an increasing problem.

Take the Midianites, a fierce and marauding band of hooligans who used to swoop down on Israelite crops and livestock, destroying and stealing at will. Israel was already doing a poor job of getting established in the land promised to them, without the distraction of home invasions. Like people everywhere, the Israelites had a bad habit of forgetting that they had pledged themselves to God and picking up their independence once again. When they did, God would take his hand of protection off them and let people like the Midianites have a field day.

Then Israel would cry out to the Master they had forgotten about, and he would send a rescuer. One such savior of the people was a man named Gideon, an unlikely prospect, considering the fact that he was a wheat farmer, not a warrior. One day, an angel went to visit him and declared, "Mighty hero, the Lord is with you!" (Judges 6:12).

Gideon did a double take, probably uttered a "Who? Me?" then asked the obvious question: Why had God forgotten them and let the Midianites do all that damage?

The angel spoke for God to such an extent that he could be called "the Lord," as if he were God himself. "Then the Lord turned to him and said, 'Go with the strength you have and rescue Israel from the Midianites. I am sending you!'" (Judges 6:14). Right. Go with the strength you have. Gideon was a wheat farmer. There was no strength there. So Gideon and the angel had words:

"I'm just a weakling."

"But the Lord will go with you."

"I don't trust you. Show me some kind of sign that all this is true."

And so on . . .

Gideon finally decided to follow the angel's command and break down all the idols in the settlement, nearly getting himself killed by his fellow Israelites for doing so. Then, in a moment of weakness, he asked for a couple more miraculous signs. Clearly this man was not hero material.

What was God thinking, choosing a Gideon instead of a real soldier? As a matter of fact, things got worse for Israel when Gideon actually pulled together an army to fight the Midianites. God told him he had *too many* men. Too many? Yes. Putting the candidates through a series of tests, God made Gideon cut his forces down to a mere three hundred soldiers, a ridiculously puny force against an enemy like this. To compound the craziness, God instructed Gideon to give each man a trumpet and an earthen pitcher with a torch burning inside it. Sure, they probably had swords too, but swords would have little value when the trumpets and pitchers were as much as hands could hold.

The whole adventure was going south really fast. Anyone could see that. But Gideon, now convinced, decided to follow God's orders to the letter. In the middle of the night, he put his three hundred men with all their strange gear onto the hillsides surrounding the Midianite encampment. At his signal, they broke their pitchers, exposing the lighted torches, and blew as loudly as they could on the trumpets. To the Midianites, it must have looked like a vast host of soldiers, since the enemy had no way of knowing that the three hundred were the whole troop, not just the buglers for a much larger army hidden by the darkness.

In the confusion that followed, the Midianites started killing each other, not knowing who was an enemy and who was a friend. Finally, the whole remaining Midianite force made a mad dash for the border, pursued by the soldiers Gideon had earlier cut out of his "army." The heavy casualties that followed ended the Midianite threat. Gideon likely didn't even have to strike a single blow until the enemy was on the run.

So what's the importance of Gideon's story for us? Simply this: We humans have put ourselves in a bad spot by walking away from the One who made us. This leaves us on our own, vulnerable, struggling with the challenges of life. When an obstacle faces us, it's easy to look at our personal resources, find them inadequate, and ask ourselves in despair, "What can I do about it?"

Gideon was a lot closer to God than many people, but he had bought into the same conclusion—that it all depended on him, and he wasn't up to the task. God had obviously picked the wrong man to be the general. A farmer—what was he thinking? Not stopping there, God told Gideon that the army was too big. The command was to chop it down to three hundred. Then God armed them with trumpets and torches, creating what was likely the most ridiculous military force ever put together.

It seems to me that God did everything he could to make Gideon's attack on the Midianites fail. But—get this—that was exactly his intention: to take the success or failure of the enterprise out of Gideon's hands. Gideon had little hope of beating the Midianites on his own, even with a big army, and God was determined to squeeze out any potential hope that was left by reducing that army to something silly.

God, to put it simply, wanted Gideon utterly dependent on him.

The point? Human ability is as fleeting and elusive as a snowflake. One day you're king or queen of the world. The next, you step out your front door and get hit by a bus, or cancer takes hold and no amount of money can buy the cure, or some accountant brings your empire down by proving you're cheating Uncle Sam.

We're not powerful. We're fragile. It's almost as if it didn't really depend on us at all, but on some Fate or Dark Lord who stays hidden but pulls the strings. In the midst of such vulnerability, God tells us, "There's a better way than walking through life alone and terrified. If you were utterly dependent on me, I could do amazing things through you."

True, we could make this insight an excuse to sit back and do nothing with our lives, turning the lie of personal independence on its head and proclaiming, "It all depends on God instead of me." But the reality is somewhere in between. God still needed Gideon to do his part while at the same time making it clear that Gideon's personal power or that of his "army" had little to do with the success of the enterprise, only with making the enterprise happen.

The story of Gideon presents the reality of our situation—that each of us lives and breathes and accomplishes only because God shapes our destiny. Psalm 104:27–29 puts it this way after describing God's care over the people and animals and even plants of this world:

> *These all look to you*
> *to give them their food at the proper time.*
> *When you give it to them,*
> *they gather it up;*
> *when you open your hand,*
> *they are satisfied with good things.*
> *When you hide your face,*
> *they are terrified;*
> *when you take away their breath,*
> *they die and return to the dust. (NIV)*

In the midst of the terrors of life, the vulnerability, the struggle to make it, God tells us that his plan was never to leave us out there on our own. We were made to belong to him, to find our success in him.

We were made to be in a place where he could care for us.

19

Love in a Barley Field

She was a Moabite foreigner, and she felt the stigma of it. The Moabites were a tribe distantly related to the Israelites, but they did not worship the true God, nor were they recognized as belonging to God's chosen people. Having married an Israelite in her homeland of Moab, only to have the man die, she was now on her way for the first time to Israel with her Jewish mother-in-law, Naomi. Ruth didn't need to go, but her deep love for Naomi made accompanying her to a strange land a no-brainer.

Naomi even tried to send her back home:

> But Ruth replied, "Don't ask me to leave you and turn back.
> I will go wherever you go and live wherever you live. Your
> people will be my people, and your God will be my God. I will
> die where you die and will be buried there. May the Lord punish
> me severely if I allow anything but death to separate us!" (Ruth
> 1:16–17)

By the time they got to Israel, it was plain that Naomi had been out of the country far too long. While she had relatives still living there, like Boaz the rich farmer, and while she had some property of her own, she had little hope of a secure life. It was barley harvesting time, so Ruth went to Boaz's fields to join the gleaners.

Gleaning was a custom authorized by the law God had given to Israel. Since there were always poor people in the land, the grain farmers were told to allow them to follow the harvesters and pick up what was dropped. Not a particularly noble activity, being a gleaner, but it put food on the table.

Boaz, however, had heard about Ruth, the Moabite widow who refused to be separated from her mother-in-law. He spoke kindly to her and instructed his workers to watch out for her safety and to pull additional stalks of grain out of their sheaves to leave on the ground for her. When she later reported everything to Naomi, there was great rejoicing. Naomi told her that Boaz was a close kinsman of hers, in fact, a "family redeemer."

Here's a little bit of trivia from ancient law. If a married Israelite man died before he could have children, the "family redeemer," a close relative of the dead man, could marry the widow. Any children they had would be considered to be offspring of the dead man so that his line would not die out. The downside was that such children would not be considered the real children of the family redeemer, so it took a special man to agree to take on this responsibility

In order to let Boaz know she was interested in being redeemed, Ruth went to the barley threshing area where Boaz was sleeping and lay at his feet. Let's pick up the account from the Bible there. In the middle of the night, Boaz woke up:

> *"Who are you?" he demanded.*
> *"I am your servant Ruth," she replied. "Spread the corner of*
> *your covering over me, for you are my family redeemer."*
> *"The Lord bless you, my daughter!" Boaz exclaimed. "You are*
> *showing more family loyalty now than ever by not running*
> *after a younger man, whether rich or poor. Now don't worry*
> *about a thing, my daughter. I will do what is necessary, for*
> *everyone in town knows you are an honorable woman. But there*
> *is one problem. While it is true that I am one of your family*
> *redeemers, there is another man who is more closely related to*
> *you than I am. Stay here tonight, and in the morning I will talk*
> *to him. If he is willing to redeem you, then let him marry you.*
> *But if he is not willing, then as surely as the Lord lives, I will*
> *marry you! Now lie down here until morning." (Ruth 3:9–13)*

The next day, Boaz went to see the other man who was a closer relative of Ruth's dead husband than he was. Showing great cunning, he told the man, truthfully, that Naomi was planning to sell land once owned by her dead son, and since this man was the nearest relative, he had the first option to buy the land and keep it in the family. The near relative agreed to make the purchase. Then Boaz told him, "Oh, by the

way, the land comes with the man's widow who you have to redeem."
The near relative immediately bowed out and turned the rights to the
land and Ruth over to Boaz.

So, with great rejoicing, Boaz married Ruth. Later they had a son,
one of whose descendents would be David, King of Israel.

Nice story, but what does it tell us? Let's recall an earlier chapter in
this book where we looked at the way God's footprints could be seen in
the things he did to bless human beings despite their rejection of him.

Here we have two women, alone and vulnerable, who experienced
blessing they could never have expected. Do you see the footprints of
God in their story? Consider this—Ruth, a Moabite who normally
would never have had anything to do with Israel, finds herself through
a strange series of circumstances to be the great-great-grandmother of
King David, who in turn would be the ancestor of Jesus Christ (more on
this later). Coincidence, or did God plan to have this foreign woman
become ancestor of Israel's king?

We've already seen that it was God's intention to use his chosen people to reach the world. Could it be that God's hand was on all of these
events because he wanted a non-Israelite in the lineage of Jesus to
demonstrate that Jesus would reach the whole world with God's message of hope? We read these words in Matthew 1 as the genealogy of
Jesus is listed:

> *Salmon was the father of Boaz (his mother was Rahab).*
> *Boaz was the father of Obed (his mother was Ruth).*
> *Obed was the father of Jesse.*
> *Jesse was the father of King David.*
> *David was the father of Solomon (his mother was*
> *Bathsheba, the widow of Uriah) . . .*
> *Jacob was the father of Joseph, the husband of Mary.*
> *Mary was the mother of Jesus, who is called the Messiah.*
> *(Matthew 1:5–6, 16)*

It is no coincidence that Ruth, a Gentile, a representative of the rest
of the world, is found is Jesus' line, despite the fact that women were
rarely mentioned in ancient genealogies. She is there because God,
through his invisible work in the circumstances of her life, put her there.
Her life may have seemed like a series of amazing coincidences, but
God was directing the course of it as surely as a pilot flies a plane or a
captain steers a ship.

20

Kings May Fall

A sad reality in the quest for the meaning of life is that each of us is only one mistake away from starting a hero and ending a loser. All through history, people have begun well and finished badly.

Israel had gone for several hundred years under the guidance of judges who got their directions from God. Not that it had been an easy ride. With their Creator more or less hidden from them, they tended to go for more visible security in the form of idols of wood and stone that they could see. Sometimes I'm tempted to criticize them for this, but then I think about the things we all gather around ourselves to give us security.

The other nations had kings—cruel, powerful despots who gave them prestige before other countries while fleecing and abusing their own people at every turn. Israel decided that judges were low-rent rulers and asked God for a genuine king. To be sure, a king would make them look like a real nation before their neighbors, but God was under no illusions as to what they were asking. He told Samuel, his current judge: "They don't want me to be their king any longer" (1 Samuel 8:7).

The point in having judges was to avoid entertaining despotic autocrats who would seek their own power rather than God's. Israel, however, was doing what humanity had always done—rejecting their Maker in favor of gods they could see.

Rather than arguing with them, God decided to give them what they wanted. He chose for them just the sort of man they were looking for, a fellow named Saul who stood a head taller than anyone else in the land and seemed outwardly impressive in every way. Not that Saul had everything going for him. When the time came for him to be proclaimed as king, no one could find him because he had fled and hidden himself.

True, he was found and properly proclaimed, but it wasn't a promising beginning.

This new king, provided by God under protest, started his reign not too badly, but he soon found himself in trouble. A massive force of Philistines had gathered to attack the Israelites, and Saul discovered that he wasn't allowed to go into battle until Samuel the high priest made the proper offering to God. But Samuel wasn't around.

Seven days passed while Saul chafed under the stupid rules that insisted that a sacrifice had to be made to God and that the only person allowed to perform it was the high priest. Finally, fed up, Saul offered the sacrifice himself. Just as he finished, Samuel showed up.

Not a big deal? Saul could only hope. Actually, in his impatience, the new king had committed a grave error that not only offended God but showed Saul unfit to continue the responsibilities of being king. Samuel curtly informed him that, though he might carry on his reign for some time longer (actually 42 years in total), his line would not continue the kingship because God had found someone else to rule, a "man after his own heart" (1 Samuel 13:14).

What followed was strange and tragic. Saul hung in there with his reign but grew increasingly moody, eventually falling into some sort of mental illness (the Bible explains that Saul was influenced by an evil spirit). At the same time, he became increasingly jealous of his intended successor, none other than David, finally resorting to hunting the next king down with the intent to kill him.

Years later, after receiving a mortal wound in battle, Saul convinced someone in his own forces to put him out of his pain forever, and David took his throne.

Miserable stories like Saul's seldom inspire much except pity. It seems like some people are put on this earth simply to serve as a warning to others. Yet, a lot of the meaning of life is bound up in Saul's unhappy experience.

God had told Israel they didn't need the prestige of a king. To show them how wrong they were, he chose someone who on the surface seemed to be the essence of kingly graces—Saul was taller than anyone else and showed himself to be a reasonably strong warrior. He was the kind of man the people naturally would have chosen, the kind of man you or I probably would have chosen.

So what was the problem? The problem was that only God could see the flaws on the inside of this ruler, but the people had rejected God as their king, so he didn't tell them. The whole experience creates a bunch of things to ponder:

1. We were made to be God's people, with God as our King. When we make our own way in the world, things degenerate really fast.
2. Saul himself tells us that when we cast God aside, we soon find ourselves out of our league. This man had likely grown up bigger and stronger than his peers, so that he generally got what he wanted with minimal effort. Under the direction of his Maker, his strengths could have been used in amazing ways. But Saul made a choice, probably early in life, to trust only himself and pull out from under the "burden" of being beholden to God. On his own he wasn't able to carry the day.
3. Each of us has flaws inside us that blow up when we choose to go our own way without reference to God. These flaws may not get us today or tomorrow, but one day they'll mess us up royally. We were never constructed to be successful at independence.
4. God may seem to have "stupid" rules in his universe, but every one of them makes sense in the larger scheme of things. Take the "sacrifice before battle" rule. Israel in this instance was clearly outclassed by the much fiercer and better equipped Philistines. They had an opportunity to have God on their side, as he had been so many times before, but to ensure that they had properly declared to him that they were ready to be dependent on him, they had to follow a procedure that made their declaration certain. When Saul, fearful that they might get overwhelmed by Philistia, did the sacrifice himself, he was simply declaring that he didn't trust God to preserve Israel until Samuel could get there.
5. Before we second-guess God's reasons for doing things, we need to take a reality check. The reasons may not be clear to us, but we're dealing with a God who understands the big picture better than we can. This is more than a "dad knows best" kind of thing. It gets to the heart of what the Bible is saying about us, that we are fallen creatures and he is Creator God. Does he know what he's doing? Yes.

Saul had every opportunity to be a big-time king. He chose to try to be a big-time man without God. In the end, he lost everything he had hoped for.

21

Even Good Kings . . .

If Saul was a disaster, King David, the next Israelite ruler, was the best you can get.

Let's start with his humble beginnings. As a teenager, David, son of Jesse and descendent of Ruth and Boaz, was a shepherd, though a gifted one. In between bouts of killing a bear or a lion attacking his flock, he composed songs, many of which we now find in the Bible's book of Psalms. David appears to have had no desire for greatness, and he understood full well how dependent he was on the God he called Lord.

One day, the prophet-judge Samuel, on instruction from God, came to Jesse to anoint from among his sons a king to replace Saul. Most of Jesse's sons looked like promising candidates except for young David, who was the runt of the litter. But God chose youth over beauty, and David was anointed. Still too young to take up the throne, David, unknown to Saul as the next king, went into Saul's service as a harpist. Along the way, he managed to get himself into a situation that compelled him to kill a giant named Goliath.

By the time Saul caught on to the fact that David had been chosen to replace him, the ailing king was in full paranoia mode. He pursued David all over Israel, hungering to kill him. But David had God's protection, and he escaped every time.

When Saul died and the chosen one was finally crowned, you would expect that any rough edges had been knocked off this poet-shepherd. To be sure, David ruled well, driving the Philistines out of his land and, above all, taking his instructions for most things from God.

But David grew lax, as humans tend to do. One day, when he should have been out with his troops, David, wandering around the palace roof, spied a young woman bathing. He sent out inquiries and discovered that her name was Bathsheba and that she was married to one of his army officers, Uriah the Hittite. Secretly calling Bathsheba to his house, David had a relationship with her, and she got pregnant.

Big problem. Interfering with another man's marriage in the ancient world was a serious crime, and something had to be done about it quickly before the general population found out. David, in what must certainly have been the darkest act of his life, arranged to have her husband Uriah become exposed to the enemy in their next battle and killed. It was nothing less than cold-blooded murder.

No one knew except a small inner circle who would never tell. It looked like the perfect crime except that one witness was going to prove troublesome. This witness—God—sent one of his prophets, a brave man named Nathan, to visit David and tell him the following story:

> *"There were two men in a certain town. One was rich, and one was poor. The rich man owned many sheep and cattle. The poor man owned nothing but a little lamb he had worked hard to buy. He raised that little lamb, and it grew up with his children. It ate from the man's own plate and drank from his cup. He cuddled it in his arms like a baby daughter. One day a guest arrived at the home of the rich man. But instead of killing a lamb from his own flocks for food, he took the poor man's lamb and killed it and served it to his guest." (2 Samuel 12:1–4)*

David was outraged and promised that this man would pay dearly for what he had done. Imagine David's shock and horror, then, when Nathan, his face grave, announced, "You are that man!" (2 Samuel 12:7). The poor man's lamb—Bathsheba—was taken from the man who loved her, and David would pay.

So we have two kings in a row brought down by their own evil deeds. But David was not going to stay down. In a Psalm renowned for its agonizing remorse, David poured out his heart:

> *Have mercy on me, O God,*
> *because of your unfailing love.*
> *Because of your great compassion,*
> *blot out the stain of my sins.*
> *Wash me clean from my guilt.*
> *Purify me from my sin.*
> *For I recognize my shameful deeds—*

they haunt me day and night.
Against you, and you alone, have I sinned;
I have done what is evil in your sight.
You will be proved right in what you say,
and your judgment against me is just. . . .
You would not be pleased with sacrifices,
or I would bring them.
If I brought you a burnt offering,
you would not accept it.
The sacrifice you want is a broken spirit.
A broken and repentant heart, O God,
you will not despise.
(Psalm 51:1–4, 16–17)

David recognized a number of realities about himself and his deed. First, he had done wrong. Most of us would agree with that—he stole another man's wife and murdered her husband. But what is it that gives us such certainty that he did wrong? Instinct? The rules that mother taught us? The morals of our society?

All of those standards are based, or so the Bible tells us, on the fact that there is a God who has set the ultimate principles for human conduct. When God spoke to David through Nathan, David knew in an instant what he later said about God in this Psalm: "You will be proved right in what you say, and your judgment against me is just" (Psalm 51:4). God was the standard-maker, so there was no way to con him into believing no crime had been committed.

The second thing that is clear here is that David could not just go off and make a sacrifice to fix everything. True, he would eventually have to take his place with the other Israelites on the Day of Atonement to have his evil forgiven through the slaughter of an animal in his place, but a simple act of sacrifice was not enough. David knew that he couldn't hope ever again to have a place with God unless he came to God with a broken spirit, came groveling to the One who had made him.

Sure, someone like David should grovel. His deeds were despicable. But recognize he is not in a category by himself. He was human like we are. Let's take another run at what the Bible says about human beings:

- We were made in God's image to reflect his nature in our own lives and represent him before all his other creatures on earth.
- Our ancestors rejected God's design for humanity in a bid for

independence that did not make them great but ruined both their
relationship with God and their relationship with one another.

- Cutting ourselves off from God, we are ever trying to do what we
were never equipped to do—to live as if we were not made by
Another and have no responsibility to Another. The result? A man
sees a beautiful woman, takes her, and kills her husband

But that was David, and you are you. You've likely never murdered
anyone, so there's no point in making a connection between David and
yourself.

The problem is that there is a connection whether or not we want it.
What separates me from a King David may only be a matter of motive
and opportunity. Who knows what darkness lurks in my heart, your
heart, all of our hearts? If you've never done anything you're deeply
ashamed of, you're not human, because all of us know, deep down, that
we're . . .

I don't want to put the word on paper, but I need to. We're *guilty.* By
some means or other, we all know, deep inside, that we've offended
some greater authority in the universe. The search for meaning is also a
search for forgiveness, even if we lie to ourselves and deny we've ever
done anything wrong, even if we tell ourselves we have no regrets and
everything we've done is justified.

That is why David's psalm is important to us—because he has
tapped into something that is the essence of why we search for meaning in the first place. We search because we've found ourselves guilty,
because we know that this life we experience personally, despite all our
attempts to make it right, is wrong. Sure, it doesn't seem wrong all the
time, but there's enough of the negative going on to tell us that the perfect little existence we dreamed about is nothing like that in the cold
light of day.

I would like to be able to tell you to chant a mantra, meditate in
some special way, get in touch with an angel, or find your spirituality
within, but will any of these rituals do the job? The problem is that fundamentally, deep in our souls, we know we need forgiveness.

So who is going to forgive you? David, in his psalm, pointed out
that, as terrible as his deed had been against Bathsheba and Uriah, it
was God he had offended and God who had to provide the forgiveness.
Sacrifices were there to take care of the problem, but they had to be
accompanied by a broken spirit, by groveling.

Possibly you're not ready to grovel. Fair enough. All of this talk about personal darkness and guilt is a hard thing to take because we have conditioned ourselves to resist any notion that there is anything wrong with us. It's common folk wisdom that bad people only need to be reeducated to become good people. Most people are more good than bad anyway, so what's to forgive?

But when you look deep in your soul, what do you see? Honestly. What do you see? Do you see guilt, and does it disturb you?

We hunger for a lot of things in this life. But the deepest need we have is for forgiveness.

Saul cried out to no one and ended badly. David cried out to the God who made him, and God forgave him. The difference between the two men? Only one of them was willing to tell the truth about himself.

22

The Meaning of Life "Under the Sun"

One of the greatest philosophers in the Bible was Qoheleth, "the Teacher," who devoted much of the latter part of his experience on earth probing various aspects of the meaning of life.

Some people who study his book, Ecclesiastes, find him to be very pessimistic, because he sees very little in human experience that he can recommend. Let's get a taste of his approach to his world:

> *A man might have a hundred children and live to be very old.*
> *But if he finds no satisfaction in life and in the end does not*
> *even get a decent burial, I say he would have been better off*
> *born dead. I realize that his birth would have been meaningless*
> *and ended in darkness. He wouldn't even have had a name, and*
> *he would never have seen the sun or known of its existence. Yet*
> *he would have had more peace than he has in growing up to be*
> *an unhappy man. He might live a thousand years twice over but*
> *not find contentment. And since he must die like everyone*
> *else—well, what's the use? (Ecclesiastes 6:3–6)*

Clearly, Qoheleth wouldn't be much fun at a party. Someone this gloomy hardly seems worth considering in our quest for meaning. But there is another way to look at his message. Qoheleth regularly used the phrase "under the Sun" (sometimes translated "in this world"), which seems to mean something like, "out there where humans live and God isn't in the equation."

The Teacher appears to have been investigating what life is actually like for people who live under the sun. In effect, Qoheleth was exploring the choices people take in life, right up to the moment when they reach the end of those choices and reflect on them in dark moments of the night. He was exploring life without God.

"Under the sun," "in this world," life begins with promise and hope, but somehow the payoff is less than what was hoped for. It is almost as if we human beings are on a perpetual search that never finds whatever it is we are looking for. Along the way, there are lots of sights to see, lots of choices to make. But nothing proves to be the ultimate answer.

So what did Qoheleth discover as he explored life "in this world"?

> *"Everything is meaningless," says the Teacher,*
> *"utterly meaningless!"*
> *What do people get for all their hard work?*
> *Generations come and go, but nothing really changes.*
> *The sun rises and sets and hurries around to rise again.*
> *The wind blows south and north, here and there, twisting*
> *back and forth, getting nowhere. The rivers run into the sea,*
> *but the sea is never full. Then the water returns again to the*
> *rivers and flows again to the sea. Everything is so weary and*
> *tiresome! No matter how much we see, we are never satisfied.*
> *No matter how much we hear, we are not content.*
> *History merely repeats itself. It has all been done before.*
> *Nothing under the sun is truly new. What can you point to that*
> *is new? How do you know it didn't already exist long ago? We*
> *don't remember what happened in those former times. And in*
> *future generations, no one will remember what we are doing*
> *now. (Ecclesiastes 1:2–11)*

Wow! If this is how it starts, you have to wonder where it will end. Actually, for Qoheleth, his declaration that life is meaningless was only a launching point from which he could begin exploring the options available to human beings without God. In the next few chapters, Qoheleth went on a search for something to take people out of the doldrums and into meaning.

Why not start with gaining wisdom? People have been visiting gurus on mountaintops for centuries to find the way to live wisely. But this is what the Teacher had to say about the search for wisdom:

> *I devoted myself to search for understanding and to explore by*
> *wisdom everything being done in the world. I soon discovered*
> *that God has dealt a tragic existence to the human race.*
> *Everything under the sun is meaningless, like chasing the wind.*
> *(Ecclesiastes 1:13–14)*

In the world, under the sun, finding wisdom is like chasing the wind because, without a roadmap you can be sure of, one person's wisdom is another person's foolishness. How do you know when you've found genuine wisdom? Nothing is certain. It's like having someone tell you that the meaning of life is 42.

If not wisdom, then how about pleasure? The Teacher tried that out too:

> *I said to myself, "Come now, let's give pleasure a try. Let's look*
> *for the 'good things' in life." But I found that this, too, was*
> *meaningless. "It is silly to be laughing all the time," I said.*
> *"What good does it do to seek only pleasure?" After much*
> *thought, I decided to cheer myself with wine. While still seeking*
> *wisdom, I clutched at foolishness. In this way, I hoped to*
> *experience the only happiness most people find during their*
> *brief life in this world. (Ecclesiastes 2:1–3)*

But seeking pleasure proved as meaningless as chasing wisdom. You can only have so much fun before you tire of it and want something more significant.

Maybe hard work is the answer. It certainly was for our parents and grandparents. But the Teacher tells us:

> *So what do people get for all their hard work? Their days of*
> *labor are filled with pain and grief; even at night they cannot*
> *rest. It is all utterly meaningless. (Ecclesiastes 2:22–23)*

How about money?

> *The more you have, the more people come to help you spend it.*
> *So what is the advantage of wealth—except perhaps to watch it*
> *run through your fingers! People who work hard sleep well,*
> *whether they eat little or much. But the rich are always*

worrying and seldom get a good night's sleep.
(Ecclesiastes 5:11–12)

So was there anything that Qoheleth could praise as a possible path to real meaning? In his search for meaning the Teacher was certainly not arguing that nothing in human experience gives us any satisfaction. In fact, most of life has enough in it to keep people going, to keep them seeking for that elusive thing they most want to have. The Teacher certainly saw at least some benefit in enjoying what you have along the way:

> *Even so, I have noticed one thing, at least, that is good. It is*
> *good for people to eat well, drink a good glass of wine, and enjoy*
> *their work—whatever they do under the sun—for however long*
> *God lets them live. And it is a good thing to receive wealth from*
> *God and the good health to enjoy it. To enjoy your work and*
> *accept your lot in life—that is indeed a gift from God. People*
> *who do this rarely look with sorrow on the past, for God has*
> *given them reasons for joy. (Ecclesiastes 5:18–20)*

Yet balancing this reality is the fact that people remain dissatisfied: "Throughout their lives, they live under a cloud—frustrated, discouraged, and angry" (Ecclesiastes 5:17). Deep within is a longing for something more significant, something that tells us human beings that we are . . . what? Worthy? Valuable? Accepted? More than just an occupier of personal space?

Being "under the sun" seems to be at the heart of the problem. "Under the sun" is the world of independence, the world without God. Once God is not in the equation, there are too many voices trying to sell their vision of what is real because a single reality is gone. Go to the religion section of a bookstore and you see what people under the sun are dealing with: This book tells you to believe and get rich, that one tells you how to find your inner child, the next says, "Learn the virtues," and the one after that assures you that angels are watching over us. *Look within, look above, recite this mantra, empty your mind, fill your mind, avoid carbohydrates.* (Sorry, I just threw that last one in.).

Qoheleth would look at a scene like this and say, "Meaningless. It's all meaningless." So what, pray tell, does he offer as an alternative except pessimism? Are we all supposed to find a bridge to jump off, or does he present us with some hope?

It's in the final chapter of his book that Qoheleth, the Teacher, finally offers some advice:

> *Don't let the excitement of youth cause you to forget your*
> *Creator. Honor him in your youth before you grow old and no*
> *longer enjoy living. It will be too late then to remember him,*
> *when the light of the sun and moon and stars is dim to your old*
> *eyes, and there is no silver lining left among the clouds. . . .*
> *Yes, remember your Creator now while you are young, before*
> *the silver cord of life snaps and the golden bowl is broken. Don't*
> *wait until the water jar is smashed at the spring and the pulley*
> *is broken at the well* [all symbols of death]. *For then the dust*
> *will return to the earth, and the spirit will return to God who*
> *gave it. (Ecclesiastes 12:1–2, 6–7)*

Remembering your Creator, in the Bible's view, means more than just recalling that he exists. It means returning to him, embracing him, recognizing who he is—the Creator—and who you are—his creation. This remembrance is what snatches people out from "under the sun," and puts them into a place with signposts, a place where God is once again supreme.

And so, for the Teacher, the choice is fairly obvious. In a world without any sure path to follow, you can try everything you can think of and spend your mortal years searching for the ultimate answer to it all. But, he warns, his own experience has shown him that every proposed solution turns out to be meaningless. There is too much fog around it all, too few signposts.

When people remember their Creator, the signposts that begin appearing are more significant than all the many voices of our experience under the sun. When people remember their Creator, they find, before they die, why they live.

23

I Led You Through the Desert

King David's reign was followed by that of his son, Solomon. After his time, Israel entered into a civil dispute that split it into northern and southern kingdoms. Not wanting to trouble you with more of a history lesson than is necessary, let's just say that things went downhill from there. The northern kingdom turned away from God in favor of idols and was overrun by the Assyrians. The southern kingdom hung on for a little more than another hundred years but turned from God as well and ended up being put into exile in Babylon.

There are some who would blame all this on the Jewish people, as if they were an inferior nation that couldn't hang onto the blessing they had been given. This is a bad rap. In fact, blaming it all on the Jews misses the point of why the Bible tells their story, which is simply this— their story is our story. They are *us*—no better, no worse. When we read their history, we are supposed to see our own—that all of us started well, then caught the independence bug and went down a road we weren't equipped for.

In the middle of the southern kingdom's journey downhill toward eventual exile, a man named Jeremiah was called by God to give his people one last chance to turn back. For more than forty years, Jeremiah walked the land, proclaiming doom and judgment, reviled by most everyone, including his own family. But his was not just a message of "turn back or God will get you." It was the voice of God, the spurned Lover, seeking the answer to a heartbreaking question. Jeremiah put it this way:

The Lord gave me another message. He said, "Go and shout in Jerusalem's streets: 'This is what the Lord says: I remember how eager you were to please me as a young bride long ago, how you loved me and followed me even through the barren wilderness.

In those days Israel was holy to the Lord, the first of my children. All who harmed my people were considered guilty, and disaster fell upon them. I, the Lord, have spoken!'"

Listen to the word of the Lord, people of Jacob—all you families of Israel! This is what the Lord says: "What sin did your ancestors find in me that led them to stray so far? They worshiped foolish idols, only to become foolish themselves. They did not ask, 'Where is the Lord who brought us safely out of Egypt and led us through the barren wilderness—a land of deserts and pits, of drought and death, where no one lives or even travels?'

"And when I brought you into a fruitful land to enjoy its bounty and goodness, you defiled my land and corrupted the inheritance I had promised you." (Jeremiah 2:1–7)

The passage is a bit long, but I wanted you to experience it, to catch the essence of the grieving voice of God asking, "What sin did your ancestors find in me?" (Jeremiah 2:5). If you've been fed the story that God only wants to dominate you, to ruin your life, keep you down, prevent you from finding your true purpose, then you have been fed an illusion.

Jeremiah's prophecy takes us far away from the view of some that God may have originated the world but he has left it to its own devices ever since. The Creator reveals himself movingly as the Husband, the Lover, who led his bride Israel through the desert to a place of safety and blessing. He is referring, of course, to the years when Israel, under the direction of Moses, fled from slavery in Egypt and traveled through the wilderness to the land that God had promised them.

They would have died out there if he hadn't led them and fed them, if he hadn't protected them from their enemies and looked out for their every need. The people of Israel for a time were utterly devoted to him, knowing how much he loved them. And he was devoted to them, loving them in spite of their failings, wanting nothing more than a bond with them closer than that of husband and wife.

Then, as the Israelites took possession of their land, they fell under the influence of people with other gods, and we read that:

> *They built pagan shrines and set up sacred pillars and*
> *Asherah poles on every high hill and under every green tree.*
> (1 Kings 14:23)

They found other gods, other lovers, and to the One who made them this was the ultimate rejection, a spiritual adultery of the lowest order. God was betrayed, and it wounded him more than any unfaithful act would wound a human lover, because he had made the ones he loved. They had pledged themselves to him and had left him for false gods who had never made anything.

Israel fell into religious adultery, going after an illusion, leaving her Husband to grieve and ask the question "Why?" This isn't the so-called angry God of the Bible, the one who would rather punish than bless. This is the Lover who tells us that he made us and only wants to shower us with his goodness.

We aren't just reading the story of the Jewish people, the Bible insists. Their story is ours. "What sin," God asks, "did you find in me that led you to stray so far?" (Jeremiah 2:5a). In their defense, the response of most people, of course, would be that we were only doing what people do—trying to make meaning out of our lives, following our instincts to be, to do, and to make something of ourselves. We were just trying to make life worth something. We never actually intended to thumb our noses at God.

But Jeremiah, speaking as God's messenger, responds, "They worshiped foolish idols, only to become foolish themselves" (Jeremiah 2:5b). Idols don't have to be gods of wood and stone. They can be anything that substitutes for a relationship with God—money, self-importance, even community.

So is the Bible saying that we've made ourselves into walking disasters? Yes and no. The Bible has already given us the consistent theme that Adam and Eve's bid for independence from God diminished them, ruined them, brought them into the same misery we see in so much of life today. This leads us to the question: If creatures made only for one purpose turn around and defy that purpose, diminishing themselves, then what are they worth? The answer surely must be "not much."

But there's another side to this: God, who refused to wipe humanity off the face of the earth, who came back and wooed a special people to be his own, still loves them, no matter what damage has been done to their worth. He cares about their fate. He reaches out to them and leads them through the treacherous desert to the land he promised them. And when they turn from him again and once more make themselves worthless, he reaches out to them, not to hurt but to restore.

But this means that a darker side of our Creator had to be revealed, beyond the passionate call of the spurned Lover, because God knew his people weren't listening to him. Nothing would get their attention except an event so catastrophic that they would be driven back into his arms. Thus, the loving God became the angry God, not because anger is his main thing but because nothing but anger could save them from following their path of independence right into destruction. Nothing but anger would bring them back within the circle of his love.

Isaiah 57:15–21 expresses this strange combination of love and anger perfectly:

> *The high and lofty one who inhabits eternity, the Holy One,*
> *says this: "I live in that high and holy place with those whose*
> *spirits are contrite and humble. I refresh the humble and give*
> *new courage to those with repentant hearts. For I will not fight*
> *against you forever; I will not always show my anger. If I did,*
> *all people would pass away—all the souls I have made. I was*
> *angry and punished these greedy people. I withdrew myself from*
> *them, but they went right on sinning. I have seen what they do,*
> *but I will heal them anyway! I will lead them and comfort those*
> *who mourn. Then words of praise will be on their lips. May*
> *they have peace, both near and far, for I will heal them all," says*
> *the Lord. "But those who still reject me are like the restless sea.*
> *It is never still but continually churns up mire and dirt. There*
> *is no peace for the wicked," says my God.*

The plan of God for Israel was simple. Call it "tough love" if you want. He determined to turn the Babylonians loose on his own people to attack them and drag them into exile in a distant land. This is what he had to say about it:

> *"But now I am sending for many fishermen who will catch*
> *them," says the Lord. "I am sending for hunters who will search*
> *for them in the forests and caves. . .*
> *"So now I will show them my power and might,"*
> *says the Lord. "At last they will know that I am the Lord."*
> *(Jeremiah 16:16, 21)*

If you view God's actions as a spurned lover getting even, go ahead, but you would be wrong. We're talking about the God who made these people and who loved them utterly. This same God could not stand by and watch them ruin themselves through corruption, injustice, bloody victimization of the weak, and every other action hell-bent to make life a disaster. He had to rescue them from themselves.

Shock treatment was at the heart of his plan, for sure. When Babylon finally invaded and carted off a major portion of the people to a foreign land to live in exile, God's people woke up from their nightmare and rediscovered the purpose they had lost so long ago.

Waking up is a good thing. If you are seeking the meaning of life, you've been doing so because you haven't found it where you are. So maybe where you are isn't where you're supposed to be. Maybe you're inhabiting an explanation that is not working for you any longer. Maybe you're starting to wake up to the fact that reality is somewhere else.

It could be that the better option now lies in listening to the One who loves you most, the Lover who wants you back in the place of safety.

24

Hosea and Gomer

The theme of God as the spurned lover actually had expression many years earlier than the time of Jeremiah in the striking story of Hosea and Gomer. Hosea, a spokesman of God in the northern part of Israel, married a prostitute. This wouldn't be considered the wisest move if you wanted marital stability, especially when the woman, Gomer, had no intention of giving up her profession.

Was Hosea a fool, a glutton for punishment? No, he was under orders. This is how the Bible explains it:

> *When the Lord first began speaking to Israel through Hosea, he said to him, "Go and marry a prostitute, so some of her children will be born to you from other men. This will illustrate the way my people have been untrue to me, openly committing adultery against the Lord by worshiping other gods."*
> *So Hosea married Gomer, the daughter of Diblaim, and she became pregnant and gave Hosea a son. And the Lord said, "Name the child Jezreel, for I am about to punish King Jehu's dynasty to avenge the murders he committed at Jezreel. In fact, I will put an end to Israel's independence by breaking its military power in the Jezreel Valley." (Hosea 1:2–5)*

This was a tough mission, maybe the toughest a man could take on, to commit himself to a woman he knew would deceive him, betray him, and make him look like a fool. He would give his heart to her, and she would joke with her many lovers about his weakness and vulnerability.

Hosea and Gomer had other children after their first one, though whether or not they were actually Hosea's is an open question:

> *Soon Gomer became pregnant again and gave birth to a daughter. And the Lord said to Hosea, "Name your daughter Lo-ruhamah—'Not loved'—for I will no longer show love to the people of Israel or forgive them. But I, the Lord their God, will show love to the people of Judah. I will personally free them from their enemies without any help from weapons or armies."*
> *After Gomer had weaned Lo-ruhamah, she again became pregnant and gave birth to a second son. And the Lord said, "Name him Lo-ammi—'Not my people'—for Israel is not my people, and I am not their God." (Hosea 1:6–9)*

Clearly there is a lot of symbolism going on here. Each of the children bore a name that represented something God wanted to tell Israel. God was once again facing that curious situation in which humanity, represented by one chosen people, had gone past the point of no return in its rejection of its Maker. He knew they deserved rejection, but there seems to be a contradiction here. In one breath he said, "For I will no longer show love to the people of Israel or forgive them" (Hosea 1:6), and in the next, he promised, "But I, the Lord their God, will show love to the people of Judah" (verse 7).

"Israel" represented the northern branch of God's people, who had gone beyond his help in their craving for independence. They would be overwhelmed by the Assyrians and would cease to exist as a people. But "Judah," the southern portion of God's people, would be preserved despite the fact that they were nearly as willful in their rejection of him as the north had been. A remnant would be rescued.

It's not that God was torn between the two options—wipe them all out or love them. It's much more complicated than that, like any relationship is complicated. He couldn't, on the one hand, tolerate leaving the people the way they were. By this time, the land was full of injustice and greed. It was neither a happy place nor a successful place, just an environment of misery.

But the people, on the other hand, wouldn't listen to him and find a pathway out. Thus Hosea was chosen to be a visible reminder of what God wanted to tell Israel—that they had made a choice not to be loved by him, in fact, not to be his people at all, though he loved them with a longing clouded by anguish. Thus the northern tribes would be lost, but he would save the south.

He declared his people not to be his people any longer, then reversed himself with the words:

> *Yet the time will come when Israel will prosper and become a*
> *great nation. In that day its people will be like the sands of the*
> *seashore—too many to count! Then, at the place where they*
> *were told, "You are not my people," it will be said, "You are*
> *children of the living God." (Hosea 1:10)*

You can see God's desire in these words, the way he is reaching out to them, assuring them that after all the pain there will be joy when they return. In the end, a remnant of his people would be rescued, though they had rejected his rule.

Back to Hosea. Gomer eventually left him and returned to prostitution, hooking up with a pimp, or maybe she sold herself into service as a harlot in an idol temple. In any case, God told poor Hosea to go get her:

> *Then the Lord said to me, "Go and get your wife again. Bring*
> *her back to you and love her, even though she loves adultery.*
> *For the Lord still loves Israel even though the people have*
> *turned to other gods, offering them choice gifts." (Hosea 3:1)*

Love her? After what she had done? He should have left her there. She deserved nothing after first receiving his love, then rejecting his love, then turning to other lovers. But God still loved Israel, and so Hosea was ordered to live out God's experience in his own life and buy back the unfaithful wife:

> *So I bought her back for fifteen pieces of silver and about five*
> *bushels of barley and a measure of wine. Then I said to her,*
> *"You must live in my house for many days and stop your*
> *prostitution. During this time, you will not have sexual*
> *intercourse with anyone, not even with me."*
> *This illustrates that Israel will be a long time without a king or*
> *prince, and without sacrifices, temple, priests, or even idols! But*
> *afterward the people will return to the Lord their God and to*
> *David's descendant, their king. They will come trembling in*
> *awe to the Lord, and they will receive his good gifts in the last*
> *days. (Hosea 3:2–5)*

There was a price for Gomer to pay—she would no longer share Hosea's bed—even as God's people would go through many years of exile in Assyria, Egypt, and Babylon, without king or temple or even their precious idols. But in the end they would receive God's good gifts.

In Hosea's tragic story we see mirrored the heart of God. It is a heart that refuses to give up on the lost and wayward one. It is a heart that thinks nothing of paying the price to win her back.

And so, the Creator God said:

> *"For my people are determined to desert me. They call me the*
> *Most High, but they don't truly honor me.*
> *"Oh, how can I give you up, Israel? How can I let you go? . . .*
> *My heart is torn within me, and my compassion overflows. No,*
> *I will not punish you as much as my burning anger tells me to.*
> *I will not completely destroy Israel, for I am God and not a mere*
> *mortal. I am the Holy One living among you, and I will not*
> *come to destroy.*
> *"For someday the people will follow the Lord. I will roar like a*
> *lion, and my people will return trembling from the west. Like a*
> *flock of birds, they will come from Egypt. Flying like doves, they*
> *will return from Assyria. And I will bring them home again,"*
> *says the Lord. (Hosea 11:7–11)*

One day they would fly like doves from the land of exile and slavery, back into the arms of God.

25

Hope from the Most Unlikely Source

God's chosen people soon experienced seventy years of exile in Babylon, followed by a return to their homeland under the control of various external powers, including Alexander the Great. Then, following a bold rebellion, the Jewish people became fully independent for over a hundred years, only to fall under the control of Rome.

But a remnant of them had learned something from exile. Those who returned from Babylon abandoned idolatry forever and turned back to their God. Even still, over the years, political domination from foreigners and an increasingly fossilized religion turned their experience sour. By the time Jesus arrived on the scene, life was not happy for these people who remembered the glories of David's kingdom. Once again, they had lost their way, and many of them longed for renewed meaning.

What we have here is a vicious cycle of initial hope found in serving God, failure, repentance; another try at serving God, failure, repentance . . . and so on. The people never seemed to arrive anywhere where life could make sense, where they could believe they were forgiven, where they could be free of fear and doubt and meaninglessness.

But a plan was brewing, a scheme that had been in the works for centuries. More than seven hundred years before, a prophet named Isaiah had told of a Servant of the Lord, a mysterious figure that some see as the nation of Israel and others as an individual who would represent God's people and suffer on their behalf.

We could think of Isaiah's proclamation as simply a symbolic presentation of the pain of Israel's suffering, but there is good reason to understand it as the prediction of a strange answer to the struggles of all humanity—strange because it was initiated by the very one that humanity had offended the most: its Maker.

Let's have a look at what Isaiah prophesied long before the time of Jesus:

> *Who has believed our message*
> *and to whom has the arm of the Lord been revealed?*
> *He grew up before him like a tender shoot,*
> *and like a root out of dry ground.*
> *He had no beauty or majesty to attract us to him,*
> *nothing in his appearance that we should desire him.*
> *He was despised and rejected by men,*
> *a man of sorrows, and familiar with suffering.*
> *Like one from whom men hide their faces*
> *he was despised, and we esteemed him not.*
> *(Isaiah 53:1–3 NIV)*

Whoever this passage was talking about, his life was rough. He grew up like a fragile flower but had no natural beauty that would attract anyone to him. People despised and rejected him, filling his life with sorrow and suffering. They turned their faces from him and gave him no value.

Certainly, this could just be a metaphor for Israel in the midst of foreign domination, except for the next part:

> *Surely he took up our infirmities*
> *and carried our sorrows,*
> *yet we considered him stricken by God,*
> *smitten by him, and afflicted.*
> *But he was pierced for our transgressions,*
> *he was crushed for our iniquities;*
> *the punishment that brought us peace was upon him,*
> *and by his wounds we are healed.*
> *We all, like sheep, have gone astray,*
> *each of us has turned to his own way;*
> *and the Lord has laid on him*
> *the iniquity of us all.*
> *(Isaiah 53:4–6 NIV)*

This servant figure is not simply an outcast in a nasty world. He bears our evil. He carries our iniquities. All of a sudden, the servant's meaninglessly tragic life is given a purpose—to absorb the evil of the rest of us, to take our guilt on his own back.

This passage reminds me of the Day of Atonement when animals were slaughtered and the evil deeds of the people were read over a goat who took that evil on itself and was sent into the wilderness to die. When we looked earlier at this annual day of forgiveness for Israel, we saw that for Israel, the cost of their independence was death, because only blood sacrifice could pay the price.

Isaiah 53 is a prophecy about one who was to come to reconnect us with God through the sacrifice of himself. Let's look at it again:

> *We all, like sheep, have gone astray,*
> *each of us has turned to his own way;*
> *and the Lord has laid on him*
> *the iniquity of us all.*
> *(Isaiah 53:6 NIV)*

Like sheep? This is a long way from Adam and Eve in the Garden believing the lie that they could be like God if only they had the courage to defy him. The bid for independence has gone sour, and now people are reduced to being compared with sheep—obviously stupid creatures—wandering who-knows-where.

The Bible is uncompromising on this—independence from God is ruin, disaster, a destruction of the meaning we were made for. We are like sheep wandering in the wilderness, incapable of caring for ourselves.

So how would we return to God if we wanted to? The barrier between ourselves and him, constructed out of our independence, has piled up a whole lot of offenses that have to be paid for. Like the blood sacrifice of the Day of Atonement, God lays on the mysterious figure of Isaiah 53 the iniquities, the offenses, of us all. He bears our penalty, takes the price of our rebellion on himself. This servant takes on our guilt so that . . .

. . . so that maybe there is a door of forgiveness that will open, and God will be on the other side of it.

26

Light in the Darkness

I was sitting alone in a darkened room one Christmas Eve many years ago. Things had gone badly in my life for the past few months, and, in a normally snowy part of Canada, not even a blanket of white had made its appearance. I remembered earlier Christmases and that feeling of . . . of what? Of fierce joy, almost of awe, as snow fell and the whole world picked up the illusion that we were different than we are. And I remember reaching out that dark, snowless night . . . for God? I think I was grasping for reality instead of the phoniness that haunted me.

So I was sitting there in the darkness, thinking about how well it served as a metaphor for my life, when the skies opened and it started to snow, suddenly, with no warning—big, soft flakes that covered the ground like manna from heaven. It was as if a door had opened to a better place, and I felt such peace and joy that I was overwhelmed.

This is what Israel experienced. She had been chosen to be God's showpiece, to make plain to the rest of the world what life could be if human beings gave up their illusions and remembered what they were made for before they met the snake in the Garden. But Israel herself turned from God and went after false gods. By the time they got to Jesus, the Israelites had suffered under more than sixty years of Roman rule, and the people themselves had become depressed and hopeless. Sure, they had religion, but their leaders were into serving their own needs, not those of their people.

Let's get away from Israel-bashing in all this. Israel was no better, no worse than anyone else. As a people, the Israelites were only human, revealing something that we need to know if we're going to understand why we tick the way we do: When we seize life for ourselves, we can't become better people. We just increase our baggage and pile up our problems.

In the midst of our doubts about succeeding at living, any spirituality that can take us out of our narrow existence looks pretty inviting. But a spirituality tacked on to a life that has lost its roots in God is a flimsy thing that won't satisfy us in the long run. That is why, despite the religiousness of the Israelites of Jesus' time, their condition was labeled as "darkness."

Into that darkness came a man, someone more than a man, named Jesus, and a bulb went on. The gospel of Matthew put it this way:

> *The people living in darkness*
> *have seen a great light;*
> *on those living in the land of the shadow of death*
> *a light has dawned.*
> *(Matthew 4:16 NIV)*

You see, people think they're alive because they're breathing and talking and doing. They may think that all they need to fill the void in their lives is a little more spirituality, or a few angels looking after them, or a mantra to meditate on.

But humanity lives in the land of the shadow of death, cut off from the life of the One who made them. They live in the wreckage of their independence, and the words of God echo in their ears, "If you eat of its fruit, you will surely die" (Genesis 2:17). They thought they could be free of him, but now that they've walked out of his presence, they find themselves in a bad place, a very dark place.

If only someone could bring a lighted candle, just a little glimmer of understanding to replace all that humanity has lost.

Into the darkness walked Jesus.

The Bible claims he was born of a virgin. Whether you accept that or not, he is worth a second look. Born into very humble circumstances in Bethlehem about 4 B.C., he grew up as the son of a woodworker in Nazareth, a nothing town in the Galilee region. At age thirty he emerged suddenly as a dramatic speaker and miracle worker, gathering crowds of thousands who followed him everywhere. Within a few years, however, those same crowds turned on him, and he was executed on a Roman cross. Three days later, his followers reported that he had risen from the dead.

A story like that sounds like a fantastic adventure, but few people would want to build their lives on some wild legend. We're used to making a distinction between non-miraculous reality and fantasy. But maybe the world we think we know isn't exactly the world that is real. Maybe miracles do happen.

I'd like to start in a pretty unlikely spot—the time when Jesus was tested by the Devil. Picture this. Here is the adult Jesus, ready to start his work of preaching and miracle working, sent first into the desert by God to give the Devil a chance to have a go at him. The Devil? Think serpent in the Garden, the same one who led Adam and Eve to believe there was profit in defying their Maker. Let's pick up the story in the gospel of Luke:

> *Then Jesus, full of the Holy Spirit, left the Jordan River. He was led by the Spirit to go out into the wilderness, where the Devil tempted him for forty days. He ate nothing all that time and was very hungry.*
> *Then the Devil said to him, "If you are the Son of God, change this stone into a loaf of bread."*
> *But Jesus told him, "No! The Scriptures say, 'People need more than bread for their life.'" (Luke 4:1–4)*

Not having eaten a thing for forty days, Jesus started this episode with a deficit. Doctors tell us that forty days without food is pretty much the threshold after which a human starts to die, so the test that was flung at him was significant. He was starving. The Devil suggested that he turn the nearby stones into bread. Makes sense. Why not, if he was a miracle worker, turn stones into bread?

The answer was that the suggestion came from the same source who told Adam and Eve that eating the forbidden fruit would make them gods, the same one who got humanity started on the road away from God. Jesus' answer? "No way. Not if the idea comes from you." So, the Devil quickly moved on to another temptation:

> *Then the Devil took him up and revealed to him all the kingdoms of the world in a moment of time. The Devil told him, "I will give you the glory of these kingdoms and authority over them—because they are mine to give to anyone I please. I will give it all to you if you will bow down and worship me."*
> *Jesus replied, "The Scriptures say, 'You must worship the Lord your God; serve only him.'" (Luke 4:5–8)*

This time the test was more blatant, but tempting nevertheless. Jesus had come to earth in obscurity, poverty even, and the opportunity to do his work from a position of power was compelling. But Jesus resisted, because what is the difference between accepting a chance to rule the world and eating forbidden fruit so you can be like God? "There is only one God," Jesus was saying. "Worship him."

The final test came in the form of an opportunity for Jesus to show off his powers:

> *Then the Devil took him to Jerusalem, to the highest point of the*
> *Temple, and said, "If you are the Son of God, jump off! For the*
> *Scriptures say,*
> *'He orders his angels to protect and guard you.*
> *And they will hold you with their hands*
> *to keep you from striking your foot on a stone.'"*
> *Jesus responded, "The Scriptures also say, 'Do not test the Lord*
> *your God.'" (Luke 4:9–12)*

Jesus knew that God would take care of him no matter what. "Just do a bold stunt like jumping off the temple," the Devil suggested, "and God will rescue you and everyone will know who you are." Yet Jesus resisted again, and the Devil left him.

Interesting story, but what does it tell us about our quest for the meaning of life? Simply this: For the first time since the Fall in the Garden, a real light was shining. Here was someone who, under great temptation, stood up to the Devil and stayed true to God. Here was someone who resisted the compelling call of independence and refused to cave in to it. Here was someone who was victorious over the same stumbling block that has tripped everyone else up since Genesis 1—our natural tendency to ignore God and strike out on our own. Here was someone who passed the test that Adam and everyone who followed him has failed.

Our problem lies in the tragic reality that our independence has cut us off from God, the Source of our meaning. But in Jesus we find the first sign of hope that it is possible for human beings to forsake independence and discover the purpose for which we were put on this earth.

Over the next few chapters, I'll try to introduce you to this Jesus. Pay attention to him, because in the land of darkness a light is shining.

27

The Teacher Who Challenged Everything We've Ever Learned

Even people who don't like churches seem to think a lot of Jesus. What's not to like? In an atmosphere of total acceptance of everyone who came to him, he taught peace and love and understanding, all the things we crave in our troubled world, and the only shame is that he got killed too soon. At least, this is the explanation of him that often goes around. The reality isn't even close.

Fact is, Jesus upset the apple cart every time he opened his mouth. He challenged all the basic assumptions we live by and flew in the face of most of what we would call plain common sense. What's more, he did it all with utter certainty that he was right and that the rest of the world was wrong. He was never arrogant, just very, very certain.

One of his most famous set of sayings is found in the Sermon on the Mount, preached on a plateau above the Sea of Galilee in northern Israel. The Sermon begins with a number of blessings. Here are a few examples:

> *God blesses those who realize their need for him,*
> *for the Kingdom of Heaven is given to them.*
> *God blesses those who mourn,*
> *for they will be comforted.*
> *God blesses those who are gentle and lowly,*

for the whole earth will belong to them.
God blesses those who are hungry and thirsty for justice,
for they will receive it in full. . . .
God blesses those who are persecuted because they live for God,
for the Kingdom of Heaven is theirs.
God blesses you when you are mocked and persecuted and lied
about because you are my followers. Be happy about it! Be very
glad! For a great reward awaits you in heaven. And remember,
the ancient prophets were persecuted, too.
(Matthew 5:3–6, 10–12)

Blessing for Jesus was not like living in some golden world where every pleasure can be yours for the taking. He pictured a struggling planet where people might be poor or sorrowing or persecuted, but they could still be blessed. How? By facing reality and returning to the One who made them. To follow Jesus would mean running counter to a world addicted to independence. But his followers would still be "blessed" because they would be where they were supposed to be. In the care of God, their Maker, the Giver of blessing, their needs would be met.

Jesus continued in his sermon to challenge and contradict examples of things most of us consider meaningful. For example, people justify the use of anger because it makes them feel better, and it's certainly not as bad as murdering someone. Jesus said, "You have heard that the law of Moses says, 'Do not murder. If you commit murder, you are subject to judgment.' But I say, if you are angry with someone, you are subject to judgment!" (Matthew 5:21–22). Anger, according to Jesus, was something like murder in the heart and could bring down the very judgment of God.

People justify a little lust as part of the spice of life. Jesus said, "But I say, anyone who even looks at a woman with lust in his eye has already committed adultery with her in his heart" (Matthew 5:28). So, then, Jesus was a prude, a layer down of unkeepable laws? No. He simply understood that the deed starts with the thought, and that if we are pledged to one person, our lust for another is a betrayal of our bond. Just as hatred is murder in the heart, so lust for someone who is not ours is an attack on the one to whom we are committed.

Jesus understood that we started better than this, and he saw with startling clarity that the thoughts we think bear fruit in the mess we make of relationships.

He went further. For all the pompous hypocrites who make a big deal of their positive side so that other people will be impressed, Jesus had these words:

> *Take care! Don't do your good deeds publicly, to be admired,*
> *because then you will lose the reward from your Father in*
> *heaven. (Matthew 6:1)*

To people who, like most of us, rely on our earthly "treasures" to please us and give us security, he said:

> *Don't store up treasures here on earth, where they can be eaten*
> *by moths and get rusty, and where thieves break in and steal.*
> *Store your treasures in heaven, where they will never become*
> *moth-eaten or rusty and where they will be safe from thieves.*
> *Wherever your treasure is, there your heart and thoughts will*
> *also be. (Matthew 6:19–21)*

What is this concept of storing up "treasures in heaven"? Well, it means abandoning your search for treasure on earth and following God's plan for your life regardless of how poor or rich it makes you. In other words, abandon your plans to build a personal empire and simply do what God wants you to do, thus building eternal treasure in the real but less tangible rewards that God offers.

But what if you starve here on earth in the process? Jesus had a word of encouragement regarding that fear:

> *So I tell you, don't worry about everyday life—whether you*
> *have enough food, drink, and clothes. Doesn't life consist of*
> *more than food and clothing? Look at the birds. They don't need*
> *to plant or harvest or put food in barns because your heavenly*
> *Father feeds them. And you are far more valuable to him than*
> *they are. (Matthew 6:25–26)*

There is something absolutely revolutionary here—by not worrying about yourself, you can transcend yourself and actually live your life for God. He, in turn, will make sure you have what you need. No, this is not a call to drop out of the responsibility we all have to take care of ourselves. Even the birds seek out their food. Instead it's a call to abandon our urge to spend all our time building personal security and figure out instead what God wants for our lives. It's a kick in the head to our independence, because, according to the Bible, we were never made to do independence successfully but were made to depend on God. As Jesus put it toward the end of his sermon:

> *But anyone who hears my teaching and ignores it is foolish, like a person who builds a house on sand. When the rains and floods come and the winds beat against that house, it will fall with a mighty crash. (Matthew 7:26–27)*

Success or failure in life comes as a result of listening to or ignoring the teaching that comes from God.

Jesus had more to tell his hearers:

> *You have heard that the law of Moses says, "Love your neighbor" and hate your enemy. But I say, love your enemies! Pray for those who persecute you." (Matthew 5:43–45)*

> *Stop judging others, and you will not be judged. (Matthew 7:1)*

> *You can enter God's Kingdom only through the narrow gate. The highway to hell is broad, and its gate is wide for the many who choose the easy way. But the gateway to life is small, and the road is narrow, and only a few ever find it. (Matthew 7:13–14)*

> *Not all people who sound religious are really godly. They may refer to me as "Lord," but they still won't enter the Kingdom of Heaven. The decisive issue is whether they obey my Father in heaven. (Matthew 7:21)*

Just about every time he opened his mouth, he was challenging the very things that were the foundation of the lives of his listeners and that are still true of our lives today—personal pleasure, power, money, the rightness of revenge, and, above all, our hunger for independence. In return, he offered a "narrow gate," a difficult way, in which obedience to the One who made us is the path to fulfillment and true security.

It's almost as if he were saying, "Life your way isn't working for you, is it? Why not try it my way?"

28

Who Is This Man?

I had a friend at university who was as brilliant as they come. He'd had offers from four of the top graduate schools in the United States to pursue studies in his chosen scientific field. He aced every exam with hardly any effort. Here was somebody who had his future in the bag.

One day, after he learned that I had a faith connected with Jesus, he told me, "I wish I could have what you have, but as a science student I can't get past all those miracles."

I knew exactly what he was talking about, because it had taken a lot for me to get past those miracles myself. Being a university student puts you in a realm where you tend only to accept as real what you can see and touch. To believe that miracles happen, though I'd accepted such a belief in earlier years, would have made me look like a rube from the country who didn't know any better. So I had struggled for a long time in the first stages of my college life between the faith of my youth and the doubt raised by my university environment.

But I had seen miracles myself—a little boy diagnosed permanently blind who regained his sight after people prayed for him. Others healed of cancer when they were given no hope of living. More significantly, I had watched a sunset over the Rocky Mountains and marveled at its glory. I had watched the changing seasons and marveled at their order.

It wasn't easy for me, as a student, to move beyond believing only what I could personally observe or explain. But eventually it occurred to me that if, behind all the wonder of what is, there is a Maker, then the notion of his intruding into our observable world to do things we would never expect made perfect sense. If God exists, as I had experienced that he does, then the possibility of miracles is wide open.

The Bible presents Jesus as more than a great teacher. Hand in hand with his words was a string of deeds so amazing that the whole coun-tryside of Israel was buzzing with it. Let's have a look. I'm not going to push you to believe in miracles, but you should understand that Jesus does come in a package—words and deeds.

Beginning in the second of four biblical books that recount Jesus' life—the gospel of Mark, chapter 6—we find a remarkable series of events that had the whole countryside buzzing. First, Jesus fed five thousand men plus women and children from five small loaves of bread and two fish that he broke up and distributed. The food somehow mul-tiplied in his hands (Mark 6:30–44). Long before, God himself had fed the Israelites with manna (a sort of sweet bread in the form of small flakes) from the sky as they traveled through the wilderness toward their promised land (Exodus 16), so this act of Jesus immediately had people scratching their heads at the seeming connection between the God of the Old Testament and Jesus.

In an amazing act of bravado or foolhardiness, Jesus once walked on water to reach his disciples in their boat on the Sea of Galilee. We read that his disciples thought he was a ghost and were terrified (Mark 6:49–50), likely the same reaction you or I would have had. They were utterly amazed when they saw who it really was. Gullible people? I think not.

> *By the time Jesus got to the other side of the lake on that*
> *occasion, the crowds were waiting, having brought with them*
> *their sick and disabled friends and family. Jesus healed everyone*
> *who came (Mark 6:53–56).*

A whole series of miraculous events followed: He drove an evil spir-it out of a young girl (Mark 7:24–30); healed a deaf-mute man (Mark 7:31–37); did another mass feeding with a tiny amount of food, this time for four thousand men plus women and children (Mark 8:1–13); and healed a blind man (Mark 8:22–26). Before he was done with his earth-ly work, he would still a storm (Mark 4:35–41)—something only God could do, according to the Old Testament (Psalm 148:7–8)—and raise people from the dead (Mark 5:21–43; John 11:1–44).

This era in history indeed seems to have been a magical time when God broke into a rebellious world by sending someone to fix things. If you don't believe Jesus was a miracle worker, I would challenge you to consider the reactions of the people as they saw him in action. We read that "they were completely amazed" (Mark 6:51 NIV), and "people were overwhelmed with amazement" (Mark 7:37 NIV).

The gospel of Luke, the third account of Jesus' life in the Bible, points out another reaction—as the crowds saw these wondrous deeds, they began asking, "Who are you?" We find the question repeated in Luke 7:49; 8:25; and 9:9. Finally, Jesus asked his own followers, "Who do you think I am?" and Simon Peter, one of his closest disciples, answered, "The Messiah of God."

The term *messiah* had a long history. It meant "anointed one," and referred to the common practice of anointing Israelite kings as a declaration that they were authorized and blessed by God to do their task. In later centuries before the time of Jesus, God's spokesmen began making prophecies about someone who was to come to answer the dilemma of humanity—that independence from God had made life dark and hopeless. While these prophets didn't use the word *messiah,* by the time of Jesus this term was commonly spoken among the Jews as the title of the one prophesied in the Old Testament.

The essence of the word *messiah* is found in passages like these from centuries before Jesus' time:

> *For a child is born to us, a son is given to us. And the government will rest on his shoulders. These will be his royal titles: Wonderful Counselor, Mighty God, Everlasting Father, Prince of Peace. His ever expanding, peaceful government will never end. He will rule forever with fairness and justice from the throne of his ancestor David. The passionate commitment of the Lord Almighty will guarantee this! (Isaiah 9:6–7)*

> *"For the time is coming," says the Lord, "when I will place a righteous Branch on King David's throne. He will be a King who rules with wisdom. He will do what is just and right throughout the land. And this is his name: 'The Lord Is Our Righteousness.' In that day Judah will be saved, and Israel will live in safety." (Jeremiah 23:5–6)*

For Simon Peter to say, "You are the Messiah," was to say, "You are the promised King. You are the Promised One of Isaiah 53, the One who has come to drag us up out of darkness."

We can make what we want of the miracle stories, but we can't separate the Great Teacher from the Miracle Worker. All of the accounts of

Jesus' life present him as a unit, the Teacher telling us how God wants us to live, and the Miracle Worker demonstrating that this was the Chosen One, the Messiah, the Son of God. In fact, when John the Baptist, the prophet who announced the coming of Jesus, later began to have doubts about him, Jesus pointed to his miracles as the sign that he was indeed the One sent to rescue the world:

> *John's two disciples found Jesus and said to him, "John the*
> *Baptist sent us to ask, 'Are you the Messiah we've been*
> *expecting, or should we keep looking for someone else?'"*
> *At that very time, he cured many people of their various*
> *diseases, and he cast out evil spirits and restored sight to the*
> *blind. Then he told John's disciples, "Go back to John and tell*
> *him what you have seen and heard—the blind see, the lame*
> *walk, the lepers are cured, the deaf hear, the dead are raised to*
> *life, and the Good News is being preached to the poor. And tell*
> *him, 'God blesses those who are not offended by me.'"*
> (Luke 7:20–23)

And so, the Teacher/Miracle Worker remains inseparable. If that bothers you, hold onto your feelings for a while. Let's find out what we can about this man before we make a final judgment on him.

29

Longing

Popular culture is a reflection of the things we find the most significant. It also mirrors the things that hurt us most. We see this in the message of many of our musicians who tell us that we are faltering souls, struggling to grasp meaning in the midst of meaninglessness, doing battle with many private demons and disappointments. Back in the 1960s, Simon and Garfunkel told us that it was better to be a rock or an island, because a rock doesn't feel pain and an island doesn't ever cry. Bono of U2 insists that despite all his efforts he still hasn't found what he's looking for.

In 2003, Sarah McLachlan released her amazing song "Fallen." Its message is sad and so achingly true that people are drawn to it almost against their wills. We start our lives, she sings, thinking we will build something wondrous. Then along the way we start picking up baggage, all those bits and pieces of discord that contradict our dream. Finally, one day we find that we've descended into a pit so deep, a hole so badly messed up, that there's no going back. We find ourselves fallen. One day we simply wake up to the fact that the dream is gone.

It's hard for us to deny, if we're going to be totally honest, that there is a deep and painful longing in our hearts, an aching quest that haunts us regularly, and that our musicians are only reflecting an echo of its tragedy. We want so much from this life, yet we find that experience saps the vitality out of us, leaving us gasping like fish on a beach, torn and bleeding. We are filled with despair. Sure, we hear of people who have found personal bliss, but either we don't know any of them or they turn out to have been telling lies.

It comes down to this—if it were possible for people to find what they're looking for simply by searching for it, they would have found it by now. They've certainly been looking long and hard enough. Either there is nothing out there to find (a thought too terrible to contemplate), or whatever is out there is hiding, or there are so many options that we don't know which to trust. In the meantime, our singers tell humanity's sad story, and most people's thirst is never quenched.

The real need is for someone who has some real answers, who can take searchers beyond their experience into something that will give genuine hope. But it has to be someone who cares, who is involved, who can be trusted. Jesus offered all of that and more.

He had come to a turning point in his earthly life. At the height of his popularity, his cousin John, known as John the Baptist, the prophet who had announced Jesus' coming, got arrested by the ruler of Galilee, Herod the Tetrarch. Then Herod, to please a dancing girl named Salome (it's a long story), had John beheaded, knowing full well that the Jews believed that a person, body and soul, was a unity, and to separate a man from his body was a horror show.

So Jesus became engulfed with a weight of sorrow he had never experienced before. In the midst of this we read:

> *Then Jesus said, "Let's get away from the crowds*
> *for a while and rest." There were so many people coming*
> *and going that Jesus and his apostles didn't even have time to*
> *eat. They left by boat for a quieter spot. But many people saw*
> *them leaving, and people from many towns ran ahead along the*
> *shore and met them as they landed. A vast crowd was there as*
> *he stepped from the boat, and he had compassion on them*
> *because they were like sheep without a shepherd. So he taught*
> *them many things. (Mark 6:31–34)*

Here's the scenario: Jesus wanted some space for himself and his followers, a little oasis of time to regroup, to rest, to grieve the death of John. So they crossed the Sea of Galilee to a private rest stop, only to be greeted by the crowd that had raced around the shoreline ahead of them.

A couple of things are striking here. First, Jesus had every right to be alone, to send the crowds packing, but he didn't. Second, he knew immediately what they needed.

These people had a longing, the longing of Simon and Garfunkel or U2 or whoever Sarah McLachlan is singing about. The longing of never knowing why we're here or what we're supposed to do with our broken dreams. They wanted Jesus. They needed him. Why?

Because, as Jesus saw them, they were "like sheep without a shepherd" (Mark 6:34). Sheep are utterly vulnerable. They ruin the pastures on which they graze by yanking the grass out by the roots. They wander off and can't find their way back. They're too dumb and too slow to run from predators. Jesus saw that the crowds were like that.

They were like that because they had tried to do what they've never been equipped to do—live without a shepherd. Here the decision our ancestors made in the Garden of Eden, the decision we all inherited, comes back to mock us. We are the children of Adam and Eve, as prone as they were to forget that once there was a Shepherd. We wander off into strange territory, where predators nip at us and our pasture is ruined. Sure, we know that somewhere there must be more, and the longing consumes us, but we can't find our way to the place we want to be, because we don't understand how much we need our Shepherd.

Do sheep know they're helpless without a shepherd? Probably not. They recognize it (eventually) when they're in trouble and then start wishing for better circumstances. But they don't cry out, "Give us a shepherd so we can live." They just go on being sheep. If they're ever going to find a shepherd, the shepherd is going to have to find them.

And so Jesus, grieving over the monstrous killing of his cousin, exhausted by too many people who had too many needs, this Jesus who only wanted a little while to rest, looked at the crowd and had compassion on them. He saw their longing and he reached out to them. If it were possible, he would have stretched out his hands and given the whole lot of them a hug.

In that moment, these people understood that the shepherd they never knew they needed had found them. In the moment that he turned to them in compassion, the famous celebrity whom they had been chasing was revealed to be the master they had been longing for without knowing it. And he taught them many things.

Let me tell you something that might be hard for you to take, but I'll tell you anyway: We were made to belong to God, not like a possession or a slave, but rather like a loved one. Independence is not what it's cracked up to be. Independence builds baggage, leaving us in a dark place with only our painful hunger for more to drive us on. This longing can't be stilled by finding the next spirituality. The longing ends, according to the Bible, when the shepherd finds us and we recognize him and we throw in our lot with him.

Then, into the calm of our souls, he teaches us.

30

Like a Little Child

I was getting some gas for my car one morning when I noticed a man who had pulled up at the pump opposite me. He wasn't hard to notice, because a steady stream of foul language poured out of his mouth, not directed at anything in particular but at life in general. It was a flowing ooze of ugly sound, as if he were letting his thoughts out into the environment so that whatever dark monster lived inside him could be heard.

When he had finished pumping, the man shouted something at a teenage guy in the passenger seat of his car. The teenager said to him plaintively out of the open car window, "I just wanted to listen to the radio," and the man launched into a verbal attack on the boy that left me itching to say something. I should have said something. The real tragedy was that this young guy was likely a constant victim of his father's ugliness, his experience like living in a sewer with no outlet. Anything I would have said would probably have meant nothing to the man.

I've always believed that the health of any nation or family can be measured by the way it treats its most vulnerable members—its children. If we attack those who most need our care, then this tells us that we have utterly lost our way.

God always had a special place for children. In the Old Testament, we read:

> *Children are a gift from the Lord;*
> *they are a reward from him.*
> *(Psalm 127:3)*

Those who fear [i.e., revere and honor] *the Lord are secure; he
will be a place of refuge for their children. (Proverbs 14:26)*

It's no surprise, then, that Jesus expressed the essence of his purpose
in terms of children and childhood. It happened like this:

*One day some parents brought their children to Jesus so he
could touch them and bless them, but the disciples told them not
to bother him. But when Jesus saw what was happening, he was
very displeased with his disciples. He said to them, "Let the
children come to me. Don't stop them! For the Kingdom of God
belongs to such as these. I assure you, anyone who doesn't have
their kind of faith will never get into the Kingdom of God."
Then he took the children into his arms and placed his hands on
their heads and blessed them. (Mark 10:13–16)*

Among the Israelites, having an honored person bless your child
was considered a very good thing. Blessings were considered to be real
and tangible, so that the child would actually receive a benefit. Thus
there was a group of parents who had decided to bring their children
over to the place where Jesus was teaching so that he could confer a
blessing.

But Jesus had followers who thought of themselves as the Messiah's
handlers, and their first reaction was that their master had no time for
little tikes where there was real teaching and miracle working to be
done. They passed on a firm "get lost" to these parents and their both-
ersome children, wanting to send the lot of them packing.

That would have been the end of it, except that Jesus overheard the
whole thing and got angry. How dare his followers take it upon themselves to turn children away? Far from being little nuisances, children
were what his work was all about. Why? Because, as he put it, "The
Kingdom of God belongs to such as these. I assure you, anyone who
doesn't have their kind of faith will never get into the Kingdom of God"
(Mark 10:14–15).

The word *kingdom* here refers to the rule that God had over Adam
and Eve in the Garden before they threw it away in a bid for independence. Jesus came to call people back into relationship with God, back to
what they had before they walked away from him. He wanted them to
enter the kingdom, to consider themselves citizens of the kingdom, the
place where God ruled and his people were blessed.

This kingdom, according to Jesus, belonged to those who were like children. On another occasion, Jesus said even more plainly that, unless his listeners turned from their willful independence (which he called their "sins") and became like little children, they would never enter the kingdom (Matthew 18:3). To find a place with God, to find your home with him, you need the mind of a child.

Why a child? Simply because children are vulnerable. They depend on adults for their survival and nurture. They are in a position in which independence can only hurt them, because they don't know how to live successfully without adult care.

This expresses exactly what the Bible has been saying all along about humanity—people have made a bid for freedom from God, but they have discovered that life has turned into an endless struggle to find success and meaning. Human beings never cease struggling with their own frailty and with that longing for whatever it is that remains outside their grasp.

Childhood is a vulnerable time. Because children are relatively defenseless, God has always called on his people to protect them and all the other vulnerable citizens in society. When his people forgot God's laws in this regard, he judged them for it:

> *"I will speak against those who cheat employees of their wages,*
> *who oppress widows and orphans, or who deprive the foreigners*
> *living among you of justice, for these people do not fear me,"*
> *says the Lord Almighty. (Malachi 3:5)*

Jesus echoed the same type of judgment when he said:

> *"There will always be temptations to sin, but how terrible it will*
> *be for the person who does the tempting. It would be better to be*
> *thrown into the sea with a large millstone tied around the neck*
> *than to face the punishment in store for harming one of these*
> *little ones." (Luke 17:1–2)*

God says that we are to become like little children and enter the kingdom to be ruled by him as a loving father guides his children. But what if you decided to make yourself vulnerable, to make yourself into a child, not to a society that might one day abuse you, but to a God who only asked that you place yourself in his hands? What if you believed God when he told you that independence was ruining your life and you needed to return to his kingdom as a little one, coming under his rule? That would be a big step, because you would be turning over the control of your life, indeed, all of your personal security, to someone else. How could you be sure you could trust him? God seems so unapproachable, so unknowable. How could you be sure that giving yourself to him like a defenseless child would be a smart move?

Maybe as a first step to answering that question, you should have a look at the one who was declared to be his Messiah—at Jesus. He condemned his followers for trying to deprive children of a blessing from him. Instead of rejecting them, he took these vulnerable ones into his arms, placed his hand on their heads one by one, and blessed them.

If the health of a people is measured by the way it treats its children, then maybe the wisdom of becoming vulnerable to God is measured by the tender touch of his Son. In his kingdom, could you be treated any worse than the way Jesus dealt with the children who came to him for blessing?

31

Going Home

He grew up in a wealthy family, surrounded by all the visible reminders of the inheritance he would one day share with his older brother. You would have thought he had it made, but this young man resented his father's dominance over the family, loving though it was, and wanted his freedom. Screwing up his courage one day, he asked his father if he could take his share of the inheritance right now in cash so he could strike out on his own.

The father, no doubt, was concerned, because he knew his son was a twit who had little idea how to handle himself outside the home. But the son insisted, and the father, saddened, gave him what he asked for. Filled with joy and excitement, the young man left his family and headed for the nearest big city.

For the first while, things were great. The young heir had lots of loot to spend, and he surrounded himself with the best life could offer, buying many friends and wallowing in wine, women, and song. The money flowed like water.

Then—you guessed it—he began to discover that the well had a bottom to it. Maybe he tried to cut back on his spending, but it was too late. His cash reserves ran dry, and his "friends" abandoned him. What was more, the territory he was living in experienced a severe famine so that even the wealthy were suffering. Desperate, he hired himself out to a farmer who gave him a job feeding pigs, a nasty enough occupation anyway but even more disgusting to a Jewish man who considered pigs ceremonially unclean according to the regulations of his religion.

Thus begins Jesus' famous story of the wandering son. We can easily picture this guy finally coming to the end of himself and murmuring, "What have I done?" As Jesus put it:

"When he finally came to his senses, he said to himself,
'At home even the hired men have food enough to spare, and
here I am, dying of hunger! I will go home to my father and say,
'Father, I have sinned against both heaven and you, and I
am no longer worthy of being called your son.
Please take me on as a hired man.'
So he returned home to his father." (Luke 15:17–20)

This boy wasn't as dumb as he had acted. He suspected that there was no way to return to the status he'd had as the younger son in the household he had left. But at least his father's servants weren't starving, and maybe that would be enough—that he went back to the place where he was known so he could live out his life as a stable hand, in disgrace but with a full stomach. Not knowing what exactly to expect, he headed for home.

Meanwhile, back at the ranch (I've always wanted to use that line), his father hadn't forgotten him. In fact, his father had taken up the habit of spending long hours standing and staring down the road, hoping that the next traveler coming up the lane would be his boy. We take up the story as the son comes into sight of home:

And while he was still a long distance away, his father saw him
coming. Filled with love and compassion, he ran to his son,
embraced him, and kissed him. (Luke 15:20)

Not only did his father spot him right away, proving that he had been watching for his wayward child, but he ran to him, threw his arms around him, kissed him. The lad had his speech well rehearsed:

"Father, I have sinned against both heaven and you, and I am
no longer worthy of being called your son." (Luke 15:21)

But there was no need for it. The father interrupted him to tell the servants:

"Quick! Bring the finest robe in the house and put it on him.
Get a ring for his finger, and sandals for his feet. And kill the
calf we have been fattening in the pen. We must celebrate with a
feast, for this son of mine was dead and has now returned to life.
He was lost, but now he is found." So the party began.
(Luke 15:22–24)

In the ancient world, when you visited someone you could pretty much tell how important you were by what your host fed you. A snack meant you might be a friend but you weren't a celebrity. Killing the fattened calf and having a feast meant you were a big deal, a highly honored guest, a somebody. So this son, who had blown it and returned home expecting a future of disgrace, got a feast instead. He wasn't going to have to settle for being a servant, because he was a son, once lost and now found.

The point of all this may be obvious to you, or maybe not. This account on the lips of Jesus was a parable, an ancient method of storytelling that made a significant point by telling a tale. The waiting father is God, and the wayward son . . . well, the wayward son is us. We had an opportunity to share in the pleasures of our father's household, but we wanted more. We wanted to be free and independent. We wanted— let's admit it—to kick loose and enjoy life without Daddy scowling over our shoulder. Ultimately, we thought we could shape a better life if we were out from under God's big thumb.

But we messed it up big time, something so predictable it's amazing that we didn't see it before we fell into it. We didn't know a thing about living on our own in a distant country. We weren't equipped for survival once we had separated ourselves from our Maker, and we lacked even the most basic skills for independent life.

When we had finally sunk down as far as we could possibly go, we started wondering what it would be like to give God another try. Not that we thought we were worthy any longer of some great experience or place with him, but we had developed a longing at least to live in his household and feel safe.

Yet even while we're walking up the road back to the old homestead, we realize that Dad has been standing there all along, for agonizing days, hours, weeks, years, watching for us. And now he's running in our direction and whooping with joy as he throws his arms around us and kisses us and says, "My child, my child, I thought you were dead but you're alive. Welcome home. Join my feast. You don't have to be a slave. You were made to be my child."

It's a little overwhelming to recognize that the God we've been wondering about and the meaning we've been searching for all come down to one reality—somewhere along the way we got lost, and all God wants . . .

. . . all he wants is for us to come home.

32

He Told Me Everything I Ever Did

Jesus had ended up in the wrong part of town, in hostile territory. On his way back to Galilee from Jerusalem, where religious leaders were trying to turn the people against him, he had decided to take the short route through Samaria. The Samaritans were the last known members of the northern tribes of Israel, part Jewish and part many other Semitic peoples because of extensive intermarriage. As such, they were shunned by the rest of the Jews, and they shunned those Jews right back. There was a lot of bad blood, and the hostility could be dangerous.

The Bible describes Jesus' journey like this:

> *He had to go through Samaria on the way. Eventually he came to the Samaritan village of Sychar, near the parcel of ground that Jacob gave to his son Joseph. Jacob's well was there; and Jesus, tired from the long walk, sat wearily beside the well about noontime. (John 4:4–6)*

At the well, he met a woman who had three strikes against her. First, she was a woman (and Jewish men did not start up conversations with strange women). Second, she was a Samaritan, and, third, she had a reputation.

Still, Jesus asked her for a drink of water, and they somehow ended up in a deep conversation. She wondered why he was talking to a Samaritan woman, and he told her that if she knew who she was talking to, she could have asked for living water from him, water that was so good that she would never thirst again but would have eternal life. She had the longing, and it came out in her words:

> *"Please, sir," the woman said, "give me some of that water! Then I'll never be thirsty again, and I won't have to come here to haul water." (John 4:15)*

It was a tricky moment. Beyond normally not talking to a strange woman, a Jewish man would be in big trouble if he taught her anything without the consent of her husband. So he asked her to go get her husband and bring him back with her. Her answer was: "I don't have a husband" (John 4:17).

Once again, the uncanny comes into play. Jesus said to her, a total stranger:

> *"You're right! You don't have a husband—for you have had five husbands, and you aren't even married to the man you're living with now." (John 4:18)*

In those days, such a history would have shown her to be a loose woman, someone at the bottom of the social heap, so that merely recounting her history made Jesus look terribly judgmental. But that wasn't his purpose at all. He was telling her that he *knew*. He understood who she was, everything she had done, yet he was willing to break all the conventions of an uptight society's rules to reach out to someone like her. Why? Because he grasped instinctively the fact that she was longing for an answer to her life.

Likely feeling awkward, she diverted him into a discussion about the proper place to worship. He responded with a curious statement:

> *"But the time is coming and is already here when true worshipers will worship the Father in spirit and in truth. The Father is looking for anyone who will worship him that way. For God is Spirit, so those who worship him must worship in spirit and in truth." (John 4:23–24)*

What he meant, quite simply, was that the concept held by many Israelites that you needed to be Jewish to have a real relationship with God was passing, and now even cursed Samaritans would not have to worry about where they connected with God. Because God is a spirit, location is unimportant.

She wasn't so sure she bought all that, so she tried to divert him again:

> *The woman said, "I know the Messiah will come—the one who is called Christ. When he comes, he will explain everything to us." Then Jesus told her, "I am the Messiah!" (John 4:25–26)*

At that, she ran off to get her live-in boyfriend, telling the people of the town:

> *"Come and meet a man who told me everything I ever did! Can this be the Messiah?" (John 4:29)*

The upshot was that Jesus spent two days in this village teaching the Samaritans about himself and the things he had come to do. Many of them believed him utterly. As John's gospel puts it,

> *Then they said to the woman, "Now we believe because we have heard him ourselves, not just because of what you told us. He is indeed the Savior of the world." (John 4:42)*

To have been this kind of person in this kind of society, the Samaritan woman would have had to have been as tough as nails, enduring the constant criticism, the staring eyes, the rejection. How she had ever ended up in such a situation is a mystery, but there she was, looked down on by all.

By all but Jesus. He saw her longing. He knew she was desperately seeking the meaning of life and not finding it in the mess of her personal existence. He knew the longing of the Samaritans, cut out of the blessings that the rest of Israel were supposed to be experiencing. And he looked beyond the rules of his day that said, "Stay away from such people. Mock them or scorn them, but don't reach out to them."

Jesus reached out, and in that moment he demonstrated that he knew the Samaritans for who they were, even as they saw him for who he was—the Savior of the world.

The Samaritans weren't fools, yet they came to a startling conclusion, that this man was more than a man. How could a mere man do the things they had probably heard about him—that he fed thousands from a few loaves, walked on water, stilled a storm, raised the dead, or told a stranger the story of her life? Those who encountered him were not satisfied with seeing him as a great teacher. They knew better. This man was not from this world.

As majestic and mysterious as he was, the lowly Samaritans, used to rejection, found in Jesus someone more than a man, someone who cared enough to reach into their souls.

33

Who Killed Jesus?

It couldn't last, all this praise from the vast crowds. Jesus was too radical not to end up having the establishment of his day turn on him. His message of peace ran counter to the people's vision of a Messiah who would drive out the Romans and establish a golden age from his headquarters in Jerusalem.

By now most of the Western world, it seems, has seen Mel Gibson's film *The Passion of the Christ.* The movie opened to intense controversy. Many people labeled it anti-Semitic. Others criticized it as a Hollywood gore-fest. A lot of attendees, overwhelmed by what they had seen, found themselves at the end of the movie sitting and staring at the blank screen instead of getting up and going home. Love it or hate it, the film had an impact.

Why are so many people intrigued by the death of Jesus? One key factor is that it's hard to conceive of a reason why such a man would have to die like that. Sure, he shook people up with his teaching, but he also reached with compassion into their souls. The Bible claims that he healed virtually anyone with a need, and his message brought daylight to the darkness in which they were living.

He taught of a Father who wanted nothing more than to welcome his children home so that he could father them again. He challenged people to give up everything to follow him. He spoke of forgiving enemies. He presented an upside-down kingdom in which the meek inherit the earth.

But none of this should have earned him a conspiracy against his life, an arrest guided by a traitor, illegal trials, and condemnation by a cowardly Roman governor, leading to an execution by the cruelest means yet devised by the human heart. At his final trial, there was a fascinating interchange between that Roman governor (Pontius Pilate) and Jesus:

> *Then Pilate went back inside and called for Jesus to be brought to him. "Are you the King of the Jews?" he asked him.*
> *Jesus replied, "Is this your own question, or did others tell you about me?"*
> *"Am I a Jew?" Pilate asked. "Your own people and their leading priests brought you here. Why? What have you done?"*
> *Then Jesus answered, "I am not an earthly king. If I were, my followers would have fought when I was arrested by the Jewish leaders. But my Kingdom is not of this world."*
> *Pilate replied, "You are a king then?"*
> *"You say that I am a king, and you are right," Jesus said. "I was born for that purpose. And I came to bring truth to the world. All who love the truth recognize that what I say is true."*
> *"What is truth?" Pilate asked. (John 18:33–38)*

"What is truth?" Now there's a classic question for our age. Pilate didn't know the answer, and so he gave in to Jesus' accusers and ordered the Messiah's death.

The authorities marched him out of the city. Already horribly beaten, he was made to carry the top bar of his own cross until he could carry it no farther and someone else had to be forced to pick it up. When they arrived at Golgotha (a hill just outside Jerusalem named for its shape—the "place of the skull") they laid him down on the cross, nailed him to it through his wrist bones and his feet, then raised it up and dropped it with sickening force into its hole. There he hung in the blazing sun while the blood flowed out of his body.

If the most sadistic person on earth had wanted to devise the most fiendish torture imaginable, he could not have done better than crucifixion, a creation of the Romans. Beyond the pain of dangling from nails, the crucified person grew exhausted and soon began to droop. This would cause the lungs to start collapsing, and, in order to breathe, the victim would have to push himself back up by bracing on the nail through his feet. He might hang there for a day or two before he stopped being able to hold himself up and suffocated. Sometimes, the Romans would speed up the process by breaking the crucified person's legs with a mallet so that the lungs would collapse early.

There were two thieves crucified with him, one on each side. Maybe they deserved to be there. One of them shouted curses at the man in the middle. The other one rebuked his partner in crime:

> *But the other criminal protested, "Don't you fear God*
> *even when you are dying? We deserve to die for our evil deeds,*
> *but this man hasn't done anything wrong." Then he said,*
> *"Jesus, remember me when you come into your Kingdom."*
> *(Luke 23:40–42)*

What did the one criminal see that the other didn't? Was there something in Jesus' manner, some aura around him? I think this thief saw truth beyond anything that the religious leaders of the country had grasped—that this was no mere man and that the brutality of the crucifixion was not an end for Jesus but a transition into a new beginning. So, against all the understanding of most everyone else, this thief turned his head toward Jesus and said, "Jesus, remember me when you come into your Kingdom" (Luke 23:42).

What kingdom? There didn't seem to be any hope of a kingdom to come into, not for Jesus. Jesus was doomed, about to expire, done with this life. We can get as outraged as we want about what had happened to him, but we can't deny the fact, can we, that he was a dead man? Yet he turned to the thief and said, "I assure you, today you will be with me in paradise" (Luke 23:43). Either he was out of his mind with pain and sorrow, or he knew something we don't.

Then, in the midst of this scene of horror, darkness fell in the middle of the day. The sun was shrouded, and a chill filled the air. Some people today say it was an eclipse. Who knows what it was?

But the darkness meant something. Remember the sacrifices God instructed the Jewish people to offer? Remember the pure goat that was slaughtered for the sins of Israel and the other one that had the rebellious actions of the people read over it before it was sent off into the desert? The gore of the Day of Atonement, when a year of rebellion was purged by blood sacrifice, had to be repeated annually in Israel. Why? Because the rebellion of humanity could not be covered over by some trivial, "I'm sorry." It took blood and death, the offering of an innocent to pay for the deeds of the guilty.

You see, it's not easy to grasp the enormity of what humanity did when it stood before its Creator and told him, "I choose not to follow you." Humanity doesn't understand what it unleashed when it simply ignored him and lived like practical atheists. Maybe some people gave him lip service, as in, "I'm searching for the god within," or "I'm just looking for a little transcendence," but they never wanted him to take control of their lives. To live as if our Maker doesn't really matter is not a trivial thing.

Thus God determined to show how serious it was by demanding a penalty of death. That is what he promised Adam and Eve, and that is what happened to them, though the death was more spiritual at first, with the physical coming later. Those animal sacrifices of ancient days were intended to represent forgiveness through blood, but they had to be repeated, and they had no power to transform the heart. Then Jesus came and offered himself.

Thus the darkness . . .

It came down to one person who could represent humanity, because unlike the rest of them, he had done nothing wrong. The Jewish leaders accused him and the Romans crucified him, and darkness fell on the land, and now we are left bewildered with the meaning of it all. Who killed him? The Jews? That has been the story in some corners of Christianity for centuries. The Romans? Obviously the nails were theirs, the cross was theirs.

But the darkness tells us both opinions are dead wrong. The Jews didn't kill Jesus, the Romans either.

When the darkness fell, this was God the Father turning away from his Son. According to Mark 15:34, Jesus cried out of the darkness, "My God, my God, why have you forsaken me?" The darkness came because all that humanity had ever done to reject, ignore, and defy the God who made them, all of that fell upon him. He took the blame for all I had done and became a bloody sacrifice in my place so that I could go free.

It had been prophesied centuries before:

> *But he was wounded and crushed for our sins. He was beaten*
> *that we might have peace. He was whipped, and we were healed!*
> *All of us have strayed away like sheep. We have left God's paths*
> *to follow our own. Yet the Lord laid on him the guilt and sins of*
> *us all. (Isaiah 53:5–6)*

Later, one of Jesus' followers, Simon Peter, would echo those words in his description of Jesus' death:

> *You have been healed by his wounds! Once you were wandering*
> *like lost sheep. But now you have turned to your Shepherd, the*
> *Guardian of your souls. (1 Peter 2:24–25)*

Another follower, the apostle Paul, put it this way:

> *We urge you, as though Christ himself were here pleading with*
> *you, "Be reconciled to God!" For God made Christ, who never*
> *sinned, to be the offering for our sin, so that we could be made*
> *right with God through Christ. (2 Corinthians 5:20–21)*

If God could have spared us from judgment without letting His Son die, then He would have. But the blood of a perfect representative of the human race had to be shed, or God would simply be making light of his solemn warning to Adam and Eve that when they struck out for independence, they would die. Jesus was willing to take my guilt in his body and shed his blood as the final sacrifice for all I had done, all I will ever do.

Later, the book of Hebrews, written by an early follower of Jesus, would put it this way:

> *Those yearly sacrifices reminded them of their sins year after*
> *year. For it is not possible for the blood of bulls and goats to take*
> *away sins. . . .*
> *And what God wants is for us to be made holy by the sacrifice of*
> *the body of Jesus Christ once for all time. (Hebrews 10:3–4, 10)*

There it is. One sacrifice forever. Jesus, by shedding his own blood, by the Bible's own testimony purged the guilt all of us bore for our failed bid at independence. One sacrifice to break down the barrier between ourselves and God, so that we could go home.

As I am writing this, by a strange coincidence it is early morning on Good Friday. I am seeing in my mind this Jesus, the One who insisted that no one should stop the little children from coming to him to be blessed. The One who healed the sick and calmed the storm and raised the dead. I see Jesus, who did not go down the road of independence, who did nothing wrong.

In the darkness, they arrest him after a traitor kisses his cheek. In the darkness, they put him on trial illegally, a kangaroo court to end all kangaroo courts. I see them beat him, flesh shredding, blood spurting. I see the Roman authorities wash their hands of him. I see him, bloody and wrecked, forced to carry his cross until he can do it no longer. I hear the nails being driven into his body, the thud of the cross in its hole.

I see him hanging there, in agony and blinding thirst, yet stopping to murmur, "Father, forgive them, for they do not know what they are doing" (Luke 23:34 NIV). I see him turning in mercy to the thief who deserved to be there and assuring him, against all evidence, "Today you will be with me in paradise" (Luke 23:43). I hear him crying out in the midst of the darkness, "My God, my God, why have you forsaken me?" (Matthew 27:46; Mark 15:34) as the Father turns away from the evil that he carries in his body—my evil, not his. Finally, when no more agony can be wrung from him, he utters the words, "Father, I entrust my spirit into your hands!" (Luke 23:46).

And I can't put forward the ridiculous statement that the Jews killed Jesus or that the Romans did this terrible deed. I'm the one who killed Jesus. It was because of my rebellion against a God who created me for better things. It was because of my willful independence in ignoring the One who created me and living in a way that shamed me, shamed him. It was my rebellious acts and thoughts that he took into his own body and paid for with his own blood.

Who killed Jesus? I did.

34

Not the End

They wrapped Jesus' body up tightly and laid it in a clean tomb. The Sabbath was approaching, and his Jewish followers were barred by law from attending to his body on the Jewish day of rest. The gospel of Matthew takes up the account:

> *Early on Sunday morning, as the new day was dawning,*
> *Mary Magdalene and the other Mary went out to see the tomb.*
> *Suddenly there was a great earthquake, because an angel of the*
> *Lord came down from heaven and rolled aside the stone and sat*
> *on it. His face shone like lightning, and his clothing was as*
> *white as snow. The guards shook with fear when they saw him,*
> *and they fell into a dead faint.*
> *Then the angel spoke to the women. "Don't be afraid!" he said.*
> *"I know you are looking for Jesus, who was crucified. He isn't*
> *here! He has been raised from the dead, just as he said would*
> *happen. Come, see where his body was lying. And now, go*
> *quickly and tell his disciples he has been raised from the dead,*
> *and he is going ahead of you to Galilee. You will see him there.*
> *Remember, I have told you." (Matthew 28:1–7)*

What we have here is nothing less than testimony to the resurrection of Jesus. The women came to the tomb on Sunday morning only to find it empty despite the fact that the Romans had put a guard in front of it. According to the story, an angel had frightened them so much that the soldiers had passed out. That same angel came back to tell the women that Jesus was not there any longer. He was risen. The place where he lay was empty.

This is just the sort of thing you might suspect of a good legend. A bright young voice rises up, people flock to him and put their hopes and dreams on him. Then the bright young voice makes some enemies who manage to have him executed. But his followers can't believe the dream is dead, so they "resurrect" him in their minds like an ancient Elvis sometimes seen hanging around the local gas station.

That might be a good explanation, but it doesn't wash. Up to this point I've done very little to convince you that all the striking stories in the Bible are true. I've urged you to listen to the message and suspend judgment on the truth of it. "What, after all, is truth?" you might ask with the famous Pontius Pilate.

But now we have something too important for suspended judgment, something that makes the whole story of Jesus either what it claims to be or simply a nice fable. You see, Jesus made bold claims and did amazing deeds, then he allowed himself to be killed. If there were no resurrection, then Jesus becomes part of history, part of legend, and no one has a clue whether or not he could have supported his main claim that he came from God, even that he was God.

But what if he rose from the dead?

If he rose from the dead, as inconceivable as that might be, then the rest must be true as well. The Bible claims we are not dealing with a mere man but God in human flesh, God himself somehow infused into a physical body. Mere humans cannot come back to life, after all, and then ascend into heaven. The Bible claims that Jesus did.

The one bedrock piece of evidence we have is the empty tomb. We know it was, indeed, empty. If the tomb were not empty, then the authorities would have produced Jesus' body as soon as the reports went out that he had risen from the dead. They were determined to be done with Jesus and his movement once and for all. So the tomb must have been empty. What, then, happened to the body? Let's look at some suggestions.

The simplest explanation is that the women went to the wrong tomb, one that was empty. This, of course, presents the problem that the authorities knew which one was the right one and would have produced the body. The same would have happened if someone in authority had moved the body—it would have turned up.

Maybe Jesus' followers stole the body, then made up a story about Jesus being risen. There are, unfortunately, many difficulties with this. First, these disciples had not expected Jesus to be killed, despite his many predictions that this would happen. Thus they had little time to hatch a plot to steal the body and start a new religious movement. Second, they were utterly depressed and defeated by Jesus' death. How, between Friday and Sunday morning, did they get the motivation and courage to steal the body?

Third, most of these same followers died at the hands of executioners who demanded that they deny the story that Jesus was alive. If it were a lie, do you really think every one of them would have died for it? Fourth, there was an armed guard at the tomb. Jesus' followers were fishermen and tax collectors and the like, not the kind of people who could overcome an armed guard.

Perhaps the most ingenious explanation is that Jesus didn't actually die on the cross. He just passed out. Once laid in a cool tomb, he revived and broke out, later appearing to his followers and convincing them that he had risen from the dead. This theory has been hanging around for a long time. In recent decades it has been popularized in books like *The Passover Plot; Holy Blood, Holy Grail;* and *The Da Vinci Code.* Though all of these titles are well known for their terribly flawed historical research, it is an intriguing notion—maybe Jesus didn't rise from the dead because he wasn't actually dead.

But consider the obstacles. While it is true that he was on the cross only a few hours, he had been brutally beaten several times before he went to the cross. Crucifixion itself was no picnic, and, according to the gospel accounts (and ancient Roman practice), the authorities made sure he was dead by driving a spear into his heart.

If he survived that and revived in the tomb, there was the double problem of getting out of the tightly bound grave clothes commonly used at the time and then rolling away a stone door so massive that the three women who came to the grave on Sunday morning wondered who was going to open it so they could tend to the body (Mark 16:3). Even if he got past those challenges, he still had to overcome the guards outside and then convince his followers that he had actually risen from the dead instead of merely surviving a near-death experience. With the condition he was in, a glorious resurrection just wouldn't be believable.

Why don't you think of something else, anything, that would explain what happened to the body? Go ahead and try. But I can guarantee you that whatever explanation you give, it won't wash. In the Sherlock Holmes novel *The Sign of Four*, the great detective remarked to Watson, "When you have eliminated the impossible, whatever remains, however improbable, must be the truth." The impossible in our case is finding an explanation for the empty tomb. No options are viable.

On the other hand, we have a faith that swept the ancient world in a few centuries, a faith for which countless thousands of people died, a faith based on the foundation that Jesus, the crucified One, rose from the dead. How do we explain it? Were people more gullible in those days than they are now? Not especially. Jesus' own followers didn't believe at first either that he had actually risen from the dead.

There were witnesses who saw him alive after that first Easter Sunday. Lots of them. The apostle Paul, writing scarcely twenty years after this time, had the following to say:

> I passed on to you what was most important and what had also been passed on to me—that Christ died for our sins, just as the Scriptures said. He was buried, and he was raised from the dead on the third day, as the Scriptures said. He was seen by Peter and then by the twelve apostles. After that, he was seen by more than five hundred of his followers at one time, most of whom are still alive, though some have died by now. Then he was seen by James and later by all the apostles. Last of all, I saw him, too, long after the others, as though I had been born at the wrong time. (1 Corinthians 15:3–8)

At the time Paul wrote this, a number of the witnesses were still alive and could verify what they had seen. This wasn't mass hysteria. These were ordinary people caught up in extraordinary events that they could not explain away. Somehow the bloody and defeated Jesus had risen from the dead. For forty days after that he met with, spoke to, touched, and ate with his followers, then he ascended into the skies right in front of them and disappeared from view (Acts 1:1–11).

You can still dismiss it if you want, but what if it's true? What would that mean for you? First, it would tell you that the rest of the story is likely true as well. Jesus made no bones about showing his followers that he was more than a man. The gospel writer John called him "the Word" (i.e., the message from God) and argued that he was actually God in human flesh:

> In the beginning the Word already existed. He was with God, and he was God. . . .
> So the Word became human and lived here on earth among us. He was full of unfailing love and faithfulness. And we have seen his glory, the glory of the only Son of the Father. (John 1:1, 14)

What John was saying is that Jesus is God who took on human flesh to live a perfect life in front of us, though his divine glory could not be hidden.

Second, it would mean that he is still alive. *The Da Vinci Code* puts a Jesus who was never actually dead into a situation in which he was doomed to die for real eventually. His revival was temporary. A resurrection doesn't do this. If Jesus beat death, he beat it for good. He is alive.

Third, it would turn his death into our reason for hope. Jesus made it plain long before his crucifixion that he was going to die on behalf of others and rise from the dead. His own life was flawless. Not even his enemies could pin anything on him. If he rose from the dead, having conquered death, then his most significant claim is true—that he died to pay the penalty for our rebellion against God. He died as the ultimate blood sacrifice, carrying all we had ever done on his own back, suffering for us so that we could have a way back to the One who made us.

In this last thought lies the essence of our meaning. If we were made to belong to God, if we lost our connection with him through our own bid for independence, then Jesus is the way back. Through his sacrifice, the barrier has been broken down; he is alive, and we can go home.

35

Meaning in the Here and Now

For forty days after his resurrection, Jesus appeared often to his followers, teaching them the meaning of everything they ever needed to know about life. At first they were frightened by his strange comings and goings. He would suddenly just be there in the room with them, though they could have sworn the door had been closed. But gradually they came to understand that he meant them no harm, that he really was Jesus, the very Jesus they had known before the horrible events of his crucifixion, but now transformed. They had many questions, and he taught them many things.

The apostle Paul later compiled a list of the people who had seen him:

> He was buried, and he was raised from the dead on the third day, as the Scriptures said. He was seen by Peter and then by the twelve apostles. After that, he was seen by more than five hundred of his followers at one time, most of whom are still alive, though some have died by now. Then he was seen by James and later by all the apostles. Last of all, I saw him, too, long after the others, as though I had been born at the wrong time. (1 Corinthians 15:4–8)

The sheer number of people he showed himself to is impressive.

At the end of the forty days, Jesus gathered his twelve closest followers and told them that their task was now to spread his message, the good news that anyone could experience forgiveness and a new life of relationship with God simply by giving over everything to him. Then, as the Book of Acts puts it, "He was taken up into the sky while they were watching, and he disappeared into a cloud" (Acts 1:9).

Some people think he left this world at that point, that he abandoned all of us to live on our own as best we could without him. But the Bible makes it very clear that he stayed actively involved in the lives of his followers. Let's look at an example.

As soon as those closest to Jesus began proclaiming that Jesus was alive, their enemies launched an offensive against them. When the persecution grew more intense, the followers of Jesus scattered all over the ancient world, taking their message of hope with them everywhere they went. One of the persecutors was a man named Saul, trained as a religious teacher but convinced that Jesus was a fraud whose message polluted the true religion of Judaism. He was utterly fanatical in his desire to stamp out this movement of Christ-followers (or "Christians" as they were named by their enemies). On his way to Damascus, Syria, one day to capture a group of people devoted to Jesus, Saul's whole world came crashing down around his ears:

> As he was nearing Damascus on this mission, a brilliant light
> from heaven suddenly beamed down upon him! He fell to the
> ground and heard a voice saying to him, "Saul! Saul! Why are
> you persecuting me?"
> "Who are you, sir?" Saul asked.
> And the voice replied, "I am Jesus, the one you are persecuting!
> Now get up and go into the city, and you will be told what you
> are to do." (Acts 9:3–6)

Temporarily blinded and utterly disoriented, Saul was led by those with him to a follower of Jesus who explained the new reality to him—that Jesus was indeed alive and Saul had actually been attacking the work of the God he claimed to serve. Saul that day made Jesus the master of his life and never looked back. Within a few years, having changed his name to Paul, he became a leader in spreading the message of the Risen One to the non-Jewish people of the ancient world, eventually even taking the good news to Rome, the center of the world at that time.

During his decades of telling his message to all who would listen, Paul remained convinced that Jesus was alive and actively involved in the lives of his followers. Not only had Paul encountered the risen Jesus himself, but he understood that, for those who had committed their lives to the Risen One, Jesus lived in them. In essence he had become their very life. Here is what Paul had to say about that:

> *I pray that from his glorious, unlimited resources he will give you mighty inner strength through his Holy Spirit. And I pray that Christ will be more and more at home in your hearts as you trust in him. (Ephesians 3:16–17)*

Let's unravel his meaning just a bit. Suppose you were someone who had just given his or her life to Jesus. What would happen next? First, you'd be instantly forgiven for your determined independence from God, because Jesus has died in your place. Then you'd be given what the Bible often calls "new life" or "new birth." A transformation would happen in which God's Spirit would bring Jesus to live with you, in you. You'd have a new desire to be what God made you to be, because, through your faith in Jesus, he'd be "at home in your heart."

What does this "new life" feel like? It feels like suddenly waking up in a new world and realizing that the one you've left wasn't your home. You grasp what a life of independence has done to the people around you, what it has done to you, and you start to see the world the way God sees it—as hopeless without him and utterly meaningful when independence no longer gets in the way. You've changed citizenship and taken on the values of God's country. There's something puzzling, though, about Paul's prayer. He expresses his hope that "Christ will be more and more at home in your hearts" (Ephesians 3:17). If Jesus has left this planet, how can he live in people here on earth? The answer is that his presence comes to us in the form of the "Holy Spirit."

The Holy Spirit has quite a history in the Bible. He first appeared right at the beginning in the account of the creation, where we read that, "The earth was empty, a formless mass cloaked in darkness. And the Spirit of God was hovering over its surface" (Genesis 1:2). Throughout the Bible the Spirit is found at work in many situations, often serving as a messenger to carry out the work of God. Yet he seems to have definite individuality—he's not just another name for the power of God. In essence, the Bible announces that the Holy Spirit is God, in the same way that it makes a clear statement that Jesus is God.

It is through the presence of the Holy Spirit in our lives, if we are followers of Jesus, that Jesus himself is part of our lives. Though Jesus has physically returned to a place beside God the Father, the Holy Spirit takes up residence in us and perfectly communicates Jesus to us, so that everything Jesus wants to say and do in our lives is transmitted to us by the Spirit. Jesus earlier explained it this way:

> *When the Spirit of truth comes, he will guide you into all truth.*
> *He will not be presenting his own ideas; he will be telling you*
> *what he has heard. He will tell you about the future. He will*
> *bring me glory by revealing to you whatever he receives from*
> *me. All that the Father has is mine; this is what I mean when I*
> *say that the Spirit will reveal to you whatever he receives from*
> *me. (John 16:13–15)*

Through this communication process, having the Holy Spirit within us is the same as having Jesus in us.

So much is the Spirit within the follower of Jesus that the apostle Paul referred to our bodies as the "temple" (holy and sacred dwelling place) of the Holy Spirit:

> *Or don't you know that your body is the temple of the Holy*
> *Spirit, who lives in you and was given to you by God? You do*
> *not belong to yourself, for God bought you with a high price.*
> *(1 Corinthians 6:19–20)*

This notion of Jesus living in us through the Holy Spirit might sound strange but it's not supposed to be. Remember Adam before his decision to reject his Creator and go on his own? The Bible tells us that Adam regularly used to walk with God in the cool of the day. God would take some kind of material form and the two of them would just walk and talk and share in the sort of community that must be a wonder to behold.

That's what it's like to have Jesus be at home in our hearts. No, he doesn't take a physical form, but he's always there with us through the communicating work of the Holy Spirit—when we wake up in the morning, through all the events of our day, and when we nod off at night.

We can talk to him, tell him everything. We can ask him for help and strength and wisdom and anything else we need. While he's no vending machine dispensing everything our heart desires, he does answer our prayers and guide us through life. We may not hear an audible voice, but it soon becomes clear that he is ready to help us in every circumstance. And he gives us joy, even in the midst of the daily struggles of life.

To conclude, if you give up control of your life to Jesus who died in your place and rose again to offer you forgiveness and a new life, he never leaves you. Through the Holy Spirit, who transmits Jesus's presence right into the center of your being, Jesus is intimately involved in your life, for you now belong to him and he wants nothing more than to stay with you forever.

You might think that all this means a life of bliss in which the independence that brought us all so much trouble is gone forever. But that would be jumping ahead a chapter. True, one day, according to the Bible, everything will be perfect. But now we live in an in-between time in which, though we who have given our lives to Jesus have new life, we are not perfect. We are people under construction, unlearning independence and seeking to discover what it means to be in relationship with God.

The apostle Paul had this to say about the process of learning to live God's way:

> *Since you have been raised to new life with Christ, set your*
> *sights on the realities of heaven, where Christ sits at God's right*
> *hand in the place of honor and power. Let heaven fill your*
> *thoughts. Do not think only about things down here on*
> *earth. . . . So put to death the sinful, earthly things lurking*
> *within you. (Colossians 3:1–2, 5)*

His words tell us that our real home is somewhere else (which Paul calls "heaven") where Jesus is, though he is also here with us through the presence of the Holy Spirit in our lives. Those who intend to live as Jesus wants them to need to set their thoughts on God's realities and God's agenda, utterly rejecting the things that once belonged to their past independence. As they do, they will experience even more of the joy and purpose that characterizes the life of a follower of Jesus.

For those who embrace the good news, the rewards are here and now in discovering that being at home with God means fulfillment and meaning far beyond anything we could imagine. It means learning to look at the world through God's eyes, seeing reality as we've never seen it before, coming to understand that most of the things we once valued are worth very little in relation to the new vision of life that God provides.

God now brings peace to the heart, a love for others that didn't seem possible before, and the ability to face the ongoing challenges of living in this fallen world with courage and with the confidence that he is always there to help and to guide.

One more feature of new life with Jesus is the fact that others around us are finding it too. Living in this troubled world, most of us experience a great longing for genuine community that will help us overcome our loneliness. What better community could there be than others who have discovered the meaning of everything in Jesus? Thus being a follower of the Risen One is not just an isolated exercise—it draws us into relationship with other followers, into a community that the Bible calls "the church."

A lot of people want a spirituality that works for them but they don't warm to the idea of binding themselves into an organization with rules and restrictions. When I use the term "church," however, I'm not referring to a specific religious organization, but to a community of people transformed by Jesus and wanting to hang together to share in the joy of its common experience of having found God and meaning and everything they were looking for. Such communities exist all over the globe and are joyous attacks on loneliness. Finding true fellowship means that I have the privilege of sharing my experience of Jesus with others. Paul had much to say about such community:

> *We are all one body, we have the same Spirit,*
> *and we have all been called to the same glorious future. . . .*
> *Then we will no longer be like children, forever changing our*
> *minds about what we believe because someone has told us*
> *something different or because someone has cleverly lied to us*
> *and made the lie sound like the truth. Instead, we will hold to*
> *the truth in love, becoming more and more in every way like*
> *Christ, who is the head of his body, the church. Under his*
> *direction, the whole body is fitted together perfectly. As each*
> *part does its own special work, it helps the other parts grow, so*
> *that the whole body is healthy and growing and full of love.*
> *(Ephesians 4:4, 14–16)*

Finding "home" for the follower of Jesus is more than discovering a relationship with God, as significant as that is. It is coming to the realization that our commitment to Jesus has put us into a community comprised of all the other people who have discovered their meaning in him. That community is not something we have to create. It already exists because of our common relationship with Jesus. In such an environment, we can share together in praising the One who made us. Such communities are all around you, and they are nothing like the stereotypes you may have heard.

Instead, when you become part of such a body, it feels like coming home.

36

The End Is Better than the Beginning

The longing continues to whisper in our ears. It comes to us in the middle of the day, telling us that what we have isn't enough, that there has to be more than this. It wakes us in the night to speak to us of our loneliness, to remind us that we are not connected, to urge us to find . . .

To find what? Or who? The Bible tells us that we're looking for God. Our search has always been for God.

In the face of humanity's longing, God came to us in the form of his Son, Jesus, who died to draw us back to our Creator, and lives again to be the One who matters most to us. In the face of our longing, the One who made us offers us the answer—home, a relationship with him where we need never again be alone.

To experience home as a spiritual reality might seem like enough, but home would be even more incredibly blessed if it were tangible, like the first Garden of Eden where God and humanity walked together in the cool of the day. If you crave more than a spiritual experience and want a real and permanent setting where you can meet with the One who made you, I have very good news. Beyond this world is another one, more glorious than this one by far. Let me introduce it to you with a story from the life of Jesus.

One day while Jesus was actively involved in teaching his followers, someone came to him with news that his dear friend Lazarus, many miles away, was extremely ill. Rather than rushing over to heal him, Jesus delayed several days and Lazarus died. When Jesus finally got to the home of his friend, Lazarus's sister was really upset—if Jesus had only hurried, she told him, Lazarus could have been healed. Did Jesus care nothing for his friend? Jesus' answer, given with great love, turned her complaint on its head:

> *"I am the resurrection and the life. Those who believe in me,*
> *even though they die like everyone else, will live again. They are*
> *given eternal life for believing in me and will never perish."*
> *(John 11:25–26)*

When Jesus raised Lazarus from the dead, it was almost an anticlimax, because the words he had just uttered were so revolutionary. Those who believe in him (give their lives to him because he died for them) may die physically, but they will live again, in a state of eternal life, forever forgiven, forever at home with God in a place that is tangible and real.

The apostle Paul tells us more about the nature of this "resurrection" that all followers of Jesus will experience:

> *But someone may ask, "How will the dead be raised? What kind*
> *of bodies will they have?" . . . Our earthly bodies, which die and*
> *decay, will be different when they are resurrected, for they will*
> *never die. Our bodies now disappoint us, but when they are*
> *raised, they will be full of glory. They are weak now, but when*
> *they are raised, they will be full of power. They are natural*
> *human bodies now, but when they are raised, they will be*
> *spiritual bodies. For just as there are natural bodies, so also*
> *there are spiritual bodies. (1 Corinthians 15:35, 42–44)*

Exactly what a "spiritual body" may be isn't exactly clear, but the essence of it is found in the reality that, when it comes to the resurrected body, disappointment and weakness will be replaced by glory and power. This will be a body that cannot break down, a body fit for the other world to which God is calling us.

The promise of resurrection and eternal life isn't universal, though. There are still many people in our world who are determined to hang onto their independence and not give allegiance to the One who made them. Tragically, their death will only confirm what their life had earlier declared—that they didn't see a need for God. For these people, the afterlife will be characterized by eternal separation from the One they rejected.

But those who give their lives to the risen Jesus, the provider of eternal life, face an eternal future, beyond this world, that is amazingly bright. Free from the limitations of a weak and faltering physical form here on earth, they will have new, indestructible spiritual bodies, without pain and sorrow and all those difficulties that make human life so troubling. They will experience joy in the presence of Jesus who died and lives for them.

It sounds like some wild dream, but that is only because most of us have not experienced the realm beyond this one where God rules. If you were to visit that other world beyond our own, you would never again doubt him, never again believe that the meaning of life is simply that it's short and painful and then you die. The most amazing desire in the heart of God is that he wants to take us to his realm to live there forever. Nothing in all his plan for humanity matters more to him.

The last book of the Bible is Revelation, penned by the apostle John, who was cruelly exiled to a small island off the coast of Turkey. This book is filled with astounding prophecies about the end of this world and the beginning of another one. Through a series of visions, John saw the final triumph of God over the forces of evil that will come at the end of our age. In the midst of everything that troubles us, the Book of Revelation gives us a glimpse of a better home where we can live forever when the current one passes from the scene.

The world could end in any number of ways—a giant meteorite could wipe out all life, a new ice age could freeze us out of existence, or we could do ourselves in with global warming or thermonuclear war.

But the Bible has a different vision—God himself will undo everything we know and transform it into a new home free of pain. For the people who have given up their independence to find their true meaning in Jesus, here is hope of a new and better world in which they can find all that they've longed for.

This is how John put it:

> *Then I saw a new heaven and a new earth, for the old heaven and the old earth had disappeared. And the sea was also gone. And I saw the holy city, the new Jerusalem, coming down from God out of heaven like a beautiful bride prepared for her husband.*
> *I heard a loud shout from the throne, saying, "Look, the home of God is now among his people! He will live with them, and they will be his people. God himself will be with them. He will*

> *remove all of their sorrows, and there will be no more death or sorrow or crying or pain. For the old world and its evils are gone forever." (Revelation 21:1–4)*

We could try to unravel all the details of this prophecy, attempt to figure out what "Jerusalem" means or where it is, or how all of these strange events are going to come about, but that's not really the point. What we need to take from John's prophecies is the certain hope that God will finally undo all the disasters we have brought upon our world through our independence and restore the home from which our ancestors were driven.

The end of everything for those who belong to Jesus is a new heavens and a new earth, a life without sorrow, pain, or evil, in a place where God can live with his creation like he intended to do before we walked away from him. Jesus himself put it this way:

> *"Don't be troubled. You trust God, now trust in me. There are many rooms in my Father's home, and I am going to prepare a place for you. If this were not so, I would tell you plainly. When everything is ready, I will come and get you, so that you will always be with me where I am." (John 14:1–3)*

The grand hope of the Bible is that one day Jesus will return to take us to our true home forever. Some people call this "heaven," some "eternal life." The what and where are important, but not as crucial as the reality: that where he is we will be—always. No death, no aging, but a forever of joy and contentment with him.

The early followers of the risen Jesus faced incredible opposition. What was it that kept them going when they were persecuted and hunted down all over the Roman Empire? It was the hope that any day the evil would end and they would be with the One who loved them, in a place of utter contentment forever.

The apostle Paul spoke of it like this:

> *For we know in part and we prophesy in part, but when perfection comes, the imperfect disappears. When I was a child, I talked like a child, I thought like a child, I reasoned like a child. When I became a man, I put childish ways behind me. Now we see but a poor reflection as in a mirror; then we shall see face to face. (1 Corinthians 13:9–12 NIV)*

Paul recognized that everything in this life is immature. Everything is partial, like looking in a cloudy mirror and seeing only a murky reflection staring back at you. When we get to God's realm, we will finally see clearly.

The book of Hebrews described the hope like this:

> *For here we do not have an enduring city, but we are looking for the city that is to come. (Hebrews 13:14 NIV)*

The apostle Jude affirmed:

> *To him who is able to keep you from falling and to present you before his glorious presence without fault and with great joy—to the only God our Savior be glory, majesty, power and authority, through Jesus Christ our Lord, before all ages, now and forevermore! Amen. (Jude 1:24–25 NIV)*

Jude's expectation was that God could preserve the followers of Jesus through all the trials of life and one day take them home, calling them into his presence with great joy, there in the place where God dwells, the God who deserves all glory, majesty, power, and authority for what he has done for us through Jesus Christ.

That was the hope that kept the earlier followers of Jesus going, even as their persecutors were doing their utmost to wipe them all from the face of the earth. What do you think it could do for you?

So why doesn't Jesus return now and take us to that other world? Why have two thousand years passed, and who knows how many more to come? Here's a question for you in return—if he came today, would you be ready for him, your independence abandoned in favor of recognizing him as the One who matters most? Even if you can say "yes" to that, would your friends be ready, your family?

The apostle Paul said this about God's delay:

> *Don't you realize how kind, tolerant, and patient God is with you? Or don't you care? Can't you see how kind he has been in giving you time to turn from your sin? (Romans 2:4)*

God is not delaying the return of Jesus because he wants us to suffer a little more here in this world, but because he's not ready to wrap it all up while there are still people who are clinging to their independence and are due to miss out on the fabulous future he has waiting for those who give their lives to him. His delay is kindness, tolerance, patience.

But this should not be understood as a lack of will to pull the plug. Our world has gone so terribly wrong that it can't be rescued without remaking it. That is why John, there in exile on the Island of Patmos, was given his vision of a new heavens and a new earth that will replace the fallen one in which we live.

The promise is real, our hope is secure. The Bible never casts an ounce of doubt that everything will end with God's people, both those alive at the time and those who have died, coming home to the place that Jesus has prepared for them.

So there it is, the whole thing—the meaning of life from beginning to eternal end. Created by God for a future of joy in his presence, we abandoned our destiny in favor of one created by ourselves in the failed expectation that independence would make us happy. We lost everything in the process and ended up cut off from the One who had made us, our misery growing with every day. Then, when it seemed that things could not get any worse, God sent his own Son to die in our place, for us, and to rise from the dead to call us to give up our independence and give our lives to him.

Ahead lies eternity, the end of our longing, and in this is the promise that we will never be separated from our Creator again. There is a home waiting, a place of joy and utter fulfillment, just beyond this one, a place where the One who made us waits for us to walk with him in the cool of the day.

37

If You Want to Find Your Way . . .

The message of the Bible isn't nearly as hard to understand as some people make it out to be, but it challenges the very heart of whatever meaning we've made for ourselves while we've lived our own lives and formed our own spirituality. The Bible tells us that no self-made spiritual experience, no matter how powerful or sincere, will lift us into that other world where real life may be found. The apostle Paul put it this way:

> *God's way seems foolish to the Jews because they want a sign from heaven to prove it is true. And it is foolish to the Greeks because they believe only what agrees with their own wisdom. So when we preach that Christ was crucified, the Jews are offended, and the Gentiles say it's all nonsense. But to those called by God to salvation, both Jews and Gentiles, Christ is the mighty power of God and the wonderful wisdom of God. This "foolish" plan of God is far wiser than the wisest of human plans, and God's weakness is far stronger than the greatest of human strength. (1 Corinthians 1:22–25)*

The Bible tells us that we are broken, ruined by a desire for independence that took us away from the One who made us and that left us unable to function on our own. The prophet Isaiah in the Old Testament had a vision of what would be the final destiny of human beings without God, and it's frightening how close it seems to scenes you can watch any day on CNN:

> *The city writhes in chaos; every home is locked to keep out*
> *looters. Mobs gather in the streets, crying out for wine. Joy has*
> *reached its lowest ebb. Gladness has been banished from the*
> *land. The city is left in ruins, with its gates battered down.*
> *Throughout the earth the story is the same—like the stray olives*
> *left on the tree or the few grapes left on the vine after harvest,*
> *only a remnant is left. . . .*
> *The earth has broken down and has utterly collapsed.*
> *Everything is lost, abandoned, and confused. The earth staggers*
> *like a drunkard. It trembles like a tent in a storm.*
> (Isaiah 24:10–13, 19–20)

We can't chart a way back because we have separated ourselves from God, and the only thing that will pay for such a deed is death—ours or that of someone who stands in our place. To this point I have not emphasized the *S* word—*sin*—because it is so misunderstood. But I raise it now because the Bible does. The apostle Paul, an early opponent of Jesus' followers who changed his mind (or had it changed for him) wrote this about Jesus: "God made him who had no sin to be sin for us, so that in him we might become the righteousness of God" (2 Corinthians 5:21 NIV).

Jesus, who knew nothing of independence from God, who lived his whole life doing the will of his Father, became "sin" for us, bearing all that we had done in his own body, so that we might become the "righteousness of God." What is righteousness? Not what you might think—some kind of perfect, untouchable state in which you never do a wrong thing again. *Righteousness* means forgiveness and cleansing—being made right with God.

What it means is going back to the original plan for which he made us—to belong to him as a child belongs to a loving parent. It means experiencing the joy of knowing his constant presence in our lives as we live out the purposes for which he created human beings. Ultimately, it means being freed of the loneliness that comes when human beings abandon their Maker in favor of an independence that leads nowhere but down.

I suppose you can think about what we've discovered in the Bible and put it into your mental library of nice things to know about spirituality, but the Bible itself doesn't really allow its message just to sit there as one option among many. Jesus himself was uncompromising on this issue. He put it this way: "I am the way and the truth and the life. No one comes to the Father except through me" (John 14:6 NIV).

His point was not to throw dirt on everyone else's religion or to sneer at whatever you find spiritual in your life. Yet his claim that he is the only way to God lies at the heart of everything he came to do. You see, we can take a dose of spirituality to make us feel better or to achieve the ultimate (whatever that is), but the multitude of faiths out there do not address our fundamental problem, which is simply the fact that we have utterly alienated ourselves from God. Independence has ruined us.

Some people think the road back has to be a hard one. They imagine that God asks us to crawl a hundred miles on bleeding knees to some shrine or spend years seeking him through mystical experiences just to enter his presence. Remember what God told Adam and Eve about the forbidden fruit: "If you eat of its fruit, you will surely die" (Genesis 2:17). And die they did. So did we. We are separated from the One who gave us life. How could we imagine, then, that the road back would be easy street?

But it turns out that the road back is not a matter of what we need to do to win God's favor. In fact, God himself has already done all the work by sending his Son Jesus to earth to die for us. It cost Jesus a horror show, suspended between earth and heaven by the spikes in his hands and feet, blood dripping, darkness falling as his own Father turned his back on the evil he had become, our evil. That is why Jesus said, "No one comes to the Father except through me" (John 14:6 NIV). Simply put, no other candidate paid the price that we should have paid. There is only one road back, and it tracks through his blood.

So who is he, this Rescuer, this Savior? The early Christians puzzled over this because they were used to only one God, and now they had someone who stilled storms, raised the dead, died for the whole world, and rose from death. Who was he? Don't think they were gullible about all this. They weren't. But the conclusion became inescapable—Jesus was a man, but he was God, too. Yet there is only one God. The result was to speak of the Trinity: God is one but exists in three persons—Father, Son, and Holy Spirit.

The Bible doesn't use the word *trinity*, but the concept is described in a number of passages. Here are a couple of examples. Jesus said to his followers:

Therefore, go and make disciples of all the nations,
baptizing them in the name of the Father and the Son and the
Holy Spirit. (Matthew 28:19)

For the Jewish mind, to place the term *Father* (God) in parallel with *Son* and *Holy Spirit* was to see them as equal. Yet notice that he uses the term *name* (one entity) rather than *names* (separate beings). The apostle Paul did the same sort of thing when he wrote: "May the grace of our Lord Jesus Christ, the love of God, and the fellowship of the Holy Spirit be with you all" (2 Corinthians 13:13).

You don't have to get your head around that one just yet. But what you need to understand is that the Bible leaves no options—Jesus is more than mere man (he is God), and there is no other way out of the mess we've made of ourselves except through him. You can deny the whole thing if you want and try to convince yourself that there is nothing wrong with you or me that can't be corrected with a little meditation or some sort of spiritual pilgrimage, but the Bible says this is like a mere bandage on a mortal wound. Jesus, the risen Messiah, is the one who raises the dead. No one else can.

So how are you going to respond to all this? If you want to check it out some more, get a Bible and start with the gospel of Mark. Move on to the gospel of John and the book of Acts, key accounts of the life of Jesus and the activities of his followers after his death and resurrection. If you feel motivated, go back to the beginning and read Genesis, then the rest of the Bible.

Ask yourself if it makes sense. Does it answer your questions, not the little ones of day-to-day living, but those deep, dark ones that wake you up in the middle of the night?

Let me put the message of God's hope together in a short package: The Bible teaches that God wants one thing from you—to turn around. He wants you to tell him that your independence hasn't worked, that it has killed you, that without him you would stay in the dark forever.

He wants you to reach out to the gift he gave you when you should have had only judgment for walking away from him—Jesus, the Son, the one he sent to pay your penalty with his blood. To reach out to Jesus, the Bible calls you to confess two things—"If you confess with your mouth, 'Jesus is Lord,' and believe in your heart that God raised him from the dead, you will be saved" (Romans 10:9 NIV).

The first one is the hardest—give up your independence and declare Jesus to be Lord, the one who is in control. This flies in the face of everything we've believed, but it's the essence of the meaning of life. Simply put, we were made to be ruled by a loving God who wants to make us free of the powerful forces out there in the world of independence that were determined to ruin us. So the solution is to tell Jesus that he is in charge from now on. This, of course, recognizes that he has paved the way by paying the penalty with his blood, breaking down the barrier standing in the way of a relationship with God.

The second confession demands belief. You have to believe that Jesus is alive, not as some kind of metaphor but really, truly, and eternally alive. If you struggle with this, go back to chapter 34 and read it again. I know he is alive for a reason beyond the ones I told you about there. I know he is alive, because I did what the Bible is asking you to do, and he has utterly changed my life.

There is no way in a book this short to explain everything. Let me leave you with this: The meaning of everything is not 42. The meaning of everything lies in discovering that we were made by Someone who loves us, that we tried to free ourselves from him, that we ruined our lives, and that he sent his Son to spill his blood as payment for what we had done, then to rise from the dead to be our Lord. It lies in telling the one who died for us, "Jesus, I know you died for me and that you rose again. I surrender myself to you. Take control and give me new life."

God is the Father waiting at the gate for his wandering child. His arms are already open, long before he sees you walking toward him. On his lips are the only words you truly want to hear. He speaks:

"My child, it's time to come home."

An Invitation

If you want to discuss this further, send me an e-mail (badke@kregel.com). I might not answer people who just want to argue about religion, which is a waste of time, but if you want to ask a question or tell me what you're thinking of doing in response to the Bible's message, I'll be available. You might also want to check out my blog: http://badkemeaningofeverything.blogspot.com/.